The Book of Images

RAINER MARIA RILKE

A Bilingual Edition

Translated by Edward Snow

Revised Edition

NORTH POINT PRESS
FARRAR, STRAUS AND GIROUX
NEW YORK

North Point Press
A division of Farrar, Straus and Giroux
19 Union Square West, New York 10003

Distributed in Canada by Douglas & McIntyre Ltd.
Printed in the United States of America
First published in 1991 by North Point Press
This revised edition published in 1994

Grateful acknowledgment is made to *Massachusetts Review*,
in which "The Guardian Angel" and "Fragments from
Lost Days" first appeared.

The Library of Congress has cataloged the hardcover edition as follows:
Rilke, Rainer Maria, 1875–1926.
   [Buch der Bilder. English & German]
   The book of images / Rainer Maria Rilke ; translated
   by Edward Snow.—A bilingual ed.
      p. cm.
   I. Snow, Edward A.   II. Title.
PT2635.I652813   1991
831'.912—dc20   91-11638

ISBN-13: 978-0-86547-477-2
ISBN-10: 0-86547-477-X

Designed by David Bullen

www.fsgbooks.com

22   21   20   19   18   17   16   15   14

Contents

*First appeared in the 1906 edition of Das Buch der Bilder.

INTRODUCTION

Readers of Rilke in English are probably both more and less familiar with *The Book of Images* (*Das Buch der Bilder*) than they suppose. The volume contains a startling number of Rilke's most famous poems. "Autumn," "Lament," "The Neighbor," "Entrance," "Evening," "Childhood," "Autumn Day": these are the poems through which many readers first encounter Rilke, and become mesmerized by his work. They are also the poems that tend to epitomize what it means to characterize something—a mood, a stance, a cadence, a quality of voice, a way of looking—as "Rilkean." Indeed, it could be claimed that if *The Book of Images* were the only work we had, the Rilke we know would still exist. The poet of memory, of childhood, of leave-taking and looking-back; the poet of night and its vastnesses; the poet of human separations; the poet of thresholds and silences, of landscapes charged with remoteness and expectancy; the poet—especially—of solitude, in its endless inflections: all are to be found here, in poems as carefully proposed as anything Rilke ever wrote.

Yet taken as a whole, *The Book of Images* probably remains the least familiar of Rilke's major works. The volume has never been translated in its entirety into English. There are no book-length studies of it. Treatments of Rilke's oeuvre rarely accord it a chapter of its own. Chronologies often misplace it. Many of its most extraordinary poems—"Those of the House of Colonna," "About Fountains," and "Fragments from Lost Days," for instance—remain virtually unmentioned in literature on Rilke.

Part of the reason for this neglect must have to do with the volume's scattered, hybrid quality, which makes generalizing about it so difficult. Indeed, *The Book of Images* can seem almost studied in its variousness. Callow *jugendstil* pieces about young maidens and abandoned brides coexist with deftly poised lyrics that seek a complex relation with otherness and the outside world. And all *kinds* of poems are present. Short lyrics, dialogues, interior monologues, poems in other voices, quasi-ballads, narrative excursions into myth and history, religious poems (serious and wry), psychological portraits, a long requiem, three different poem cycles, and odd stream-of-consciousness pieces ("About Fountains," "Fragments from Lost Days") fill out the four sections of *The Book of Images*.

Such heterogeneity mirrors the circumstances in which the volume was composed. Most of Rilke's great works came into being rapidly, in short, creative bursts: twenty-six days in 1899 for the first section of *The Book of Hours*, eight days each in 1901 and 1903 for the last two sections, for a total of one hundred and thirty-five poems; most of the *New Poems* in successive summers of 1906 and 1907; all fifty-five of the *Sonnets to Orpheus* and six of the ten *Duino Elegies* in a single February of 1922. But *The Book of Images* evolved gradually, over a seven-year period (June 1899 to August 1906) that spans experiences which mark the great transition in Rilke's early life: his complicated relationship with Lou Andreas-Salomé, their two trips to Russia together, and their gradual estrangement; his stay at Worpswede, an artists' colony near Bremen where he met Clara Westhoff and Paula Becker, the two friends (one a sculptor, the other a painter) who became objects for him of dreamy, conflicted fin de siècle fantasies (such as those in the poem "Girls"); his marriage to Clara and his rejection of or by Paula, the two events obscurely related; residence in Paris, where he fell under Rodin's spell, became obsessed with a poetry of sculptural "thingness," and had his first Baudelairean experiences of inner-city estrangement; the birth of his daughter, Ruth, followed by his gradual distancing of himself from his wife and child—a sacrifice to vocation hopelessly entangled with elements of cowardice and bad faith.

Amid all this eventfulness, *The Book of Images* appeared twice, in very different versions. A first edition was published in July 1902 (Rilke was twenty-six at the time), and contained forty-five poems written between 1898 and 1901, the majority of them taken from the diaries Rilke kept at Berlin-Schmargendorfer and Worpswede. A second edition (the one translated here) appeared four years later, in December 1906, greatly altering and expanding the first. In it Rilke mixed in thirty-seven new poems, changed the order of the original sequence, deleted one poem and the final strophe of a second, gave names to untitled pieces, spliced separate poems together ("Girls," "The Son," "Charles the Twelfth of Sweden Rides in the Ukraine"), and divided the whole into two books, each with two parts.

In the period of revision between the two editions, Rilke was at work on other projects as well, putting old concerns behind him and feeling his way into new ones. The third and final section of *The Book of Hours* was written in 1903, and the completed volume was published in 1905. A second edition of the popular *Stories of God* (first published in 1900) appeared in 1904. *The Lay of the Love and Death of Cornet Christopher Rilke*, written in 1899 and a favorite whenever Rilke gave readings, was published in its final form in 1906. A monograph on Worpswede, in which concerns with landscape and painting produce intense visual description, appeared in 1903, along with the first edition of Rilke's book on Rodin, so crucial to the aesthetic of the *New Poems*. The *New Poems* themselves were begun during this period (some thirty existed by the time Rilke wrote "The Voices," the last piece composed for *The Book of Images*), and *The Notebooks of Malte Laurids Brigge*, which would not be published until 1910, had by 1906 become a major preoccupation.

It is no wonder, then, that *The Book of Images* should make such a varied impression. In a very real sense the volume spans whole phases of Rilke's career, and can be felt to trace their arc: reaching back to the art-nouveau mannerisms of the earliest poems, containing in its interstices the spirituality of *The Book of Hours*, overlapping the first of the ego-effacing *New Poems*, and pointing beyond them (in such poems as "Human Beings at Night," "The Ashanti," "Pont du Carrousel," "The Neighbor," and especially "The Voices") to *The Notebooks of Malte Laurids Brigge*, with its feelings about the city's estranging power and the unsettling presence there of God's "maimed ones." Yet at the same time *The Book of Images* seems without any agenda or unifying vision of its own (in this it differs radically from the works that surround it): its four-part structure seems arbitrarily imposed, and only emphasizes the volume as a sort of catchall, where various experiments in style, genre, subject, and voice find a place.

Not that this absence of agenda should necessarily be regretted. It makes for perhaps the most genuinely open of Rilke's works. Even the dozen or so awkward poems in *The Book of Images*—"Girls," "The Singer Sings Before a Child of Princes," and "Requiem," for example—seem revealing of Rilke the man, the young poet, in ways his earlier or later work seldom allows. Often one has the sense of Rilke writing his way into or through a poem, finding a feeling, an image, a situation, and following it wherever it leads him, not refining out what is weakest in the finished work but leaving it impure. The technique (if we can call it that) leaves Rilke painfully exposed: when nothing "comes" the result can be a kind of overwrought posturing, as in the puerile sentimentality of "Girl's Melancholy" or the sometimes effete inventiveness of "From a Stormy Night." But when the initial impulse perseveres, and against expectation finds its way into something real and unforced, the effect can be extremely moving—as in "The Blind Woman," where at some point amid the verbal thrashing-about one begins to feel the quietly evolving strength of the old woman's own confident voice. That evolution seems to take place not only in the speaker but in the poem's own texture, as it works through sentimentality and overdramatization toward some special place beyond. Several of the poems in *The Book of Images* "evolve" this way, beginning with scant promise yet coming to a haunting close. "The Son," "About Fountains," "Martyrs," "The Last Judgment," the final section of "The Tsars," the cycle "From a Stormy Night," perhaps even "The Saint" and (at the very last moment) "The Three Holy Kings": these poems can seem variously awkward, forced, tedious, or obscure, yet they all reach beautifully voiced conclusions.

In the most brilliant of the poems in *The Book of Images*, however, Rilke is uncannily confident from the first. The many great lyrics in the volume's first half seem blessed with perfect pitch. The impulse that shapes their cadences seems to come from a place so deep and so exposed that there is a complete break with the sheltered ego-lyrics of the early work. When one turns from *The Book of Hours* to the best of these poems, the change in voice is dramatic. It is as if there has been "a ripening in silence," to adapt a phrase from "Entrance." The cloistered persona, the discursive, quasi-religious manner of the former volume are cast away, and a poem like "Evening" suddenly stands free, addressing us with an immediacy and closeness not so much "spoken" as shaped from and invested with the qualities of voice:

Slowly the evening puts on the garments
held for it by a rim of ancient trees;
you watch: and the lands divide from you,
one going heavenward, one that falls;

and leave you, to neither quite belonging,
not quite so dark as the house sunk in silence,
not quite so surely pledging the eternal
as that which grows star each night and climbs—

and leave you (inexpressibly to untangle)
your life afraid and huge and ripening,
so that it, now bound in and now embracing,
grows alternately stone in you and star.

Nothing in the early work prepares us for this stately, unforced solemnity, so assured in relation to the tangle of emotions it expresses. And it is as beautifully crafted as anything in the *New Poems*. The only difference is that while the most radical of the *New Poems* exploit syntax and semantic density to achieve their version of sculptural "thingness,"[1] "Evening" works in the vocal register. Its focus may be visual, specific, oriented outward, but timing and cadence are its métier. It *shapes* voice, and this as much as anything else is what gives the poem its anti-impressionistic feeling.

Rilke chose to call this volume of poems *Das Buch der Bilder*, which can mean either a book of pictures or a book of images. I have translated

1. For a more detailed account of the sculptural analogy of the *New Poems*, see my introductions to *New Poems (1907)* (North Point Press, 1984) and *New Poems: The Other Part (1908)* (North Point Press, 1987).

it as "The Book of Images" in order not to trivialize the key term *Bild*, whose dualities are crucial to the poems. The word can designate a picture, a portrait, or any other form of pictorial representation (sculptural, architectural), and thus suggests a strong "belonging" to the visual world. But it can also designate an image that works as a metaphor—a figurative entity pointing to realities beyond or behind it. *Bilder* in this sense can populate the visual realm with traces, invisible connections, imaginings, remembrances, intimations of things lost or unrealized, waiting to be recalled or brought (back) to life.

The poems knowingly exploit these complications. The word first appears in "Girls I," which asserts that girls, unlike others (who must travel long paths to reach "the dark poets"), "don't ask / what bridge leads to images (*Bildern*)." Here the "image" connotes a desired place, a way of seeing or relating to life that requires (at least for "others") a crossing-over. But only two poems later, in "The Song of the Statue" ("*Das Lied der Bildsäule*"), the term *Bildsäule* is used to designate a statue erected on a column. Here the image is a state of imprisonment, and what is trapped there longs for "life" and "blood's rushing"—with strong implications that it once *was* life, before it was transformed into art.

The contradictions multiply in "Those of the House of Colonna," where three different uses of *Bild* are played against one another. The poem opens as the speaker views, with a mixture of admiration and envy, portraits of the noblemen of a great Italian family: "Your face is so filled with gazing, / because for you the world was picture and picture (*Bild und Bild*)." The implication is that for these Renaissance princes, with their pragmatic, world-oriented realism, the world *was* what it looked like: "out of armor, flags, ripe fruit, and women / welled for you that great confidence / that everything *is* and *counts*." But there is an irony: these men of action "stand now so motionless / in portraits (*Bildern*)," displayed forever in images that are both unnatural poses and true pictures of their self-fashioned, disciplined manhood. And that irony yields to another, as the speaker (himself a grown man) suddenly questions them about their forgotten or erased childhood, which he proceeds to recall for them in fond detail, as a time when imagination transformed or was enthralled by everything seen, when windows opened like doors upon distances, and when images engendered life in secluded places: "Back then the altar, with its painting (*Bilde*)/on which Mary gave birth, was tucked away/in the solitary side aisle." It is as if the "actual" portraits become a bridge into the realm they signify as lost forever. At the end of the poem, the speaker, having crossed that bridge, remains in the imagined "back then," still viewing the adult figures in the portraits but addressing them—with a new perspective—as "boys."

It would be an adventure to trace the exfoliations of *Bild* throughout the poems, especially as the word becomes involved with other terms of similar complexity and weight—"voice" (*Stimme*), for instance, which often seems a strange ontological category bearing little relation to its ordinary-language meanings. One of the pleasures of the volume can be exploring its "secret architecture" (to use Baudelaire's phrase), where motifs combine and recombine in intricate relations. Hand and face, for instance, are juxtaposed in the final lines of "From a Childhood" and "Those of the House of Colonna"; become a central opposition in "Prayer"; and intertwine with subtle polarities of red and white in "The Tsars" and "In the Certosa." Obviously there are nascent themes here. The play of images is a way of thinking, and even this small cluster of motifs yields paradoxes of life viewed and grasped, possessed and relinquished, lived and imagined, sacrificed and transcended, undergone and belatedly understood. But to distill from such paradoxes (which are already deductions from sensuous particulars) a set of concerns that might give the book coherence would in the end only diminish its scope, and betray the tacit dimension where images leave their meanings. Rilke himself once expressed aversion to such resolution (it was during the period when he was working on these poems), and his words might almost be those of *The Book of Images* itself:

> *I fear in myself only those contradictions with a tendency toward reconciliation. It must be a very narrow spot in my life if the idea should occur to them to shake hands, from one side to the other. My contradictions shall hear of each other only rarely and in rumors.*[2]

2. *Briefe und Tagebücher aus der Frühzeit, 1899–1902* (Leipzig: Insel, 1933), p. 203.

*

I would like to express my indebtedness to other translators of Rilke, especially J. B. Leishman, M. D. Herder Norton, Randall Jarrell, Walter Arndt, and Robert Bly. I would also like to thank Richard Howard, Edward Hirsch, and Winifred Hamilton for their many helpful suggestions about the translations and the introduction. And I owe Michael Winkler a special debt of gratitude, both for his keen insights into Rilke's language and for his generosity in sharing them with me.

The Book
of Images

The First Book, PART ONE

EINGANG

Wer du auch seist: am Abend tritt hinaus
aus deiner Stube, drin du alles weißt;
als letztes vor der Ferne liegt dein Haus:
wer du auch seist.
Mit deinen Augen, welche müde kaum
von der verbrauchten Schwelle sich befrein,
hebst du ganz langsam einen schwarzen Baum
und stellst ihn vor den Himmel: schlank, allein.
Und hast die Welt gemacht. Und sie ist groß
und wie ein Wort, das noch im Schweigen reift.
Und wie dein Wille ihren Sinn begreift,
lassen sie deine Augen zärtlich los . . .

ENTRANCE

Whoever you are: in the evening step out
of your room, where you know everything;
yours is the last house before the far-off:
whoever you are.
With your eyes, which in their weariness
barely free themselves from the worn-out threshold,
you lift very slowly one black tree
and place it against the sky: slender, alone.
And you have made the world. And it is huge
and like a word which grows ripe in silence.
And as your will seizes on its meaning,
tenderly your eyes let it go . . .

AUS EINEM APRIL

Wieder duftet der Wald.
Es heben die schwebenden Lerchen
mit sich den Himmel empor, der unseren Schultern schwer war;
zwar sah man noch durch die Äste den Tag, wie er leer war, —
aber nach langen, regnenden Nachmittagen
kommen die goldübersonnten
neueren Stunden,
vor denen flüchtend an fernen Häuserfronten
alle die wunden
Fenster furchtsam mit Flügeln schlagen.

Dann wird es still. Sogar der Regen geht leiser
über der Steine ruhig dunkelnden Glanz.
Alle Geräusche ducken sich ganz
in die glänzenden Knospen der Reiser.

FROM AN APRIL

Again the woods smell sweet.
The soaring larks lift up with them
the sky, which to our shoulders was so heavy;
true, through the boughs one still saw the day, how empty it was,—
but after long, rain-filled afternoons
come the golden sun-drenched
newer hours,
before which, on distant housefronts,
all the wounded
windows flee fearfully with beating wings.

Then it grows still. Even the rain runs more softly
over the stones' quietly darkening gleam.
All noises slip entirely away
into the brushwood's glimmering buds.

ZWEI GEDICHTE ZU HANS THOMAS SECHZIGSTEM GEBURTSTAGE

MONDNACHT

Süddeutsche Nacht, ganz breit im reifen Monde,
und mild wie aller Märchen Wiederkehr.
Vom Turme fallen viele Stunden schwer
in ihre Tiefen nieder wie ins Meer, —
und dann ein Rauschen und ein Ruf der Ronde,
und eine Weile bleibt das Schweigen leer;
und eine Geige dann (Gott weiß woher)
erwacht und sagt ganz langsam:

Eine Blonde . . .

RITTER

Reitet der Ritter in schwarzem Stahl
hinaus in die rauschende Welt.

Und draußen ist Alles: der Tag und das Tal
und der Freund und der Feind und das Mahl im Saal
und der Mai und die Maid und der Wald und der Gral,
und Gott ist selber vieltausendmal
an alle Straßen gestellt.

Doch in dem Panzer des Ritters drinnen,
hinter den finstersten Ringen,
hockt der Tod und muß sinnen und sinnen:
Wann wird die Klinge springen
über die Eisenhecke,
die fremde befreiende Klinge,
die mich aus meinem Verstecke
holt, drin ich so viele

TWO POEMS TO HANS THOMAS
ON HIS SIXTIETH BIRTHDAY

MOONLIGHT

South German night, bathed in August moonlight,
and soft as all fairytales' recurrence.
From the turret many hours fall heavily
down into their depth as into the sea,—
and then a rushing and a call from the round
and for a while the silence stays empty;
and a violin then (God knows from where)
wakes and says ever so slowly:

A blond woman . . .

KNIGHT

The knight rides forth in jet-black steel
into the rushing, turbulent world.

And outside is everything: the day and the vale
and the friend and the foe and the feast in the hall
and May and the maid and the woods and the Grail
and God himself set thousandfold
on every street.

Yet just inside the knight's armor,
behind the darkest circles,
death sits and must brood and brood:
When will the sword spring
over the iron hedge,
the strange liberating sword,
which pulls me from my
hiding-place, in which I spend

gebückte Tage verbringe, —
daß ich mich endlich strecke
und spiele
und singe.

so many hunkered days,—
so that I can finally stretch
and play
and sing.

MÄDCHENMELANCHOLIE

Mir fällt ein junger Ritter ein
fast wie ein alter Spruch.

Der kam. So kommt manchmal im Hain
der große Sturm und hüllt dich ein.
Der ging. So läßt das Benedein
der großen Glocken dich allein
oft mitten im Gebet . . .
Dann willst du in die Stille schrein,
und weinst doch nur ganz leis hinein
tief in dein kühles Tuch.

Mir fällt ein junger Ritter ein,
der weit in Waffen geht.

Sein Lächeln war so weich und fein:
wie Glanz auf altem Elfenbein,
wie Heimweh, wie ein Weihnachtsschnein
im dunkeln Dorf, wie Türkisstein
um den sich lauter Perlen reihn,
wie Mondenschein
auf einem lieben Buch.

GIRL'S MELANCHOLY

A young knight comes to mind
almost like an old saying.

He came. Thus sometimes in the grove
the great storm comes and wraps around you.
He left. Thus often the wild benison
of the great bells breaks off
in the midst of prayer . . .
Then you want to scream in the silence,
and yet only weep softly inside,
deep in your cool shawl.

A young knight comes to mind,
riding far in full armor.

His smile was so soft and fine:
like gleaming on old ivory,
like homesickness, like a Christmas snowfall
in the dark village, like turquoise
around which many pearls are fashioned,
like moonlight
on a favorite book.

VON DEN MÄDCHEN

I

Andere müssen auf langen Wegen
zu den dunklen Dichtern gehn;
fragen immer irgendwen,
ob er nicht einen hat singen sehn
oder Hände auf Saiten legen.
Nur die Mädchen fragen nicht,
welche Brücke zu Bildern führe;
lächeln nur, lichter als Perlenschnüre,
die man an Schalen von Silber hält.

Aus ihrem Leben geht jede Türe
in einen Dichter
und in die Welt.

GIRLS

I

Others must travel long paths
to reach the dark poets;
must always ask someone
if he has seen one of them singing
or placing hands on strings.
Only girls don't ask
what bridge leads to images;
only smile, brighter than pearl necklaces
ringing bowls of fine silver.

From their lives every door opens
onto a poet
and onto the world.

Mädchen, Dichter sind, die von euch lernen
das zu *sagen*, was ihr einsam *seid*;
und sie lernen leben an euch Fernen,
wie die Abende an großen Sternen
sich gewöhnen an die Ewigkeit.

Keine darf sich je dem Dichter schenken,
wenn sein Auge auch um Frauen bat;
denn er kann euch nur als Mädchen denken:
das Gefühl in euren Handgelenken
würde brechen von Brokat.

Laßt ihn einsam sein in seinem Garten,
wo er euch wie Ewige empfing
auf den Wegen, die er täglich ging,
bei den Bänken, welche schattig warten,
und im Zimmer, wo die Laute hing.

Geht! . . . es dunkelt. Seine Sinne suchen
eure Stimme und Gestalt nicht mehr.
Und die Wege liebt er lang und leer
und kein Weißes unter dunklen Buchen, —
und die stumme Stube liebt er sehr.
. . . Eure Stimmen hört er ferne gehn
(unter Menschen, die er müde meidet)
und: sein zärtliches Gedenken leidet
im Gefühle, daß euch viele sehn.

Girls, there are poets who learn from you
to *say*, what you, in your aloneness, *are*;
and they learn through you to live distantness,
as the evenings through the great stars
become accustomed to eternity.

None may ever give herself to a poet,
even if his eyes longed for women;
for he can only think of you as girls:
the feeling in your slender wrists
would break beneath brocade.

Let him be alone in his garden,
where like angels he received you—
on those paths that he wandered daily,
by those benches that wait steeped in shadows,
and in the chamber where the lute was hung.

Go! . . . it grows dark. His senses seek
your voices and shapes no longer.
And those paths he loves long and empty
and no whiteness beneath dark beech trees,—
and he loves intensely the silent room.
. . . Your voices he hears move far off
(among people, whom he wearily avoids)
and: his tender memory suffers it
like foresight, that many look on you.

DAS LIED DER BILDSÄULE

Wer ist es, wer mich so liebt, daß er
sein liebes Leben verstößt?
Wenn einer für mich ertrinkt im Meer,
so bin ich vom Steine zur Wiederkehr
ins Leben, ins Leben erlöst.

Ich sehne mich so nach dem rauschenden Blut;
der Stein ist so still.
Ich träume vom Leben: das Leben ist gut.
Hat keiner den Mut,
durch den ich erwachen will?

Und werd ich einmal im Leben sein,
das mir alles Goldenste giebt, —

— — — — — — — — — — — — — — — — — —

so werd ich allein
weinen, weinen nach meinem Stein.
Was hilft mir mein Blut, wenn es reift wie der Wein?
Es kann aus dem Meer nicht den Einen schrein,
der mich am meisten geliebt.

THE SONG OF THE STATUE

Who is there who so loves me, that he
will throw away his own dear life?
If someone will die for me in the ocean,
I will be brought back from stone
into life, into life redeemed.

How I long for blood's rushing;
stone is so still.
I dream of life: life is good.
Has no one the courage
through which I might awaken?

And if I once more find myself in life,
given everything most golden,—

— — — — — — — — — — — — — — — — — — —

then I will weep
alone, weep for my stone.
What help will my blood be, when it ripens like wine?
It cannot scream out of the ocean
he who loved me most.

DER WAHNSINN

Sie muß immer sinnen: Ich bin . . . ich bin . . .
Wer bist du denn, Marie?
   Eine Königin, eine Königin!
   In die Kniee vor mir, in die Knie!

Sie muß immer weinen: Ich war . . . ich war . . .
Wer warst du denn, Marie?
   Ein Niemandskind, ganz arm und bar,
   und ich kann dir nicht sagen wie.

Und wurdest aus einem solchen Kind
eine Fürstin, vor der man kniet?
   Weil die Dinge alle anders sind,
   als man sie beim Betteln sieht.

So haben die Dinge dich groß gemacht,
und kannst du noch sagen wann?
   Eine Nacht, eine Nacht, über *eine* Nacht, —
   und sie sprachen mich anders an.
   Ich trat in die Gasse hinaus und sieh:
   die ist wie mit Saiten bespannt;
   da wurde Marie Melodie, Melodie . . .
   und tanzte von Rand zu Rand.
   Die Leute schlichen so ängstlich hin,
   wie hart an die Häuser gepflanzt, —
   denn das darf doch nur eine Königin,
   daß sie tanzt in den Gassen: tanzt! . . .

MADNESS

She must always brood: I am . . . I am . . .
Who are you then, Marie?
   A queen, a queen!
   On your knees before me, on your knees!

She must always weep: I was . . . I was . . .
Who were you then, Marie?
   A no one's child, all poor and bare,
   and words can't say how.

And there has grown from such a child
a princess, to whom one kneels?
   Because these things all are different now
   from how one begging sees them.

So the things have made you great,
and can you still say when?
   One night, one night, all through *one* night,—
   and how they greeted me had changed.
   I stepped out into the street and . . . look:
   it is stretched as if with strings;
   then Marie grew melody, melody . . .
   and danced from edge to edge.
   The people crept past so cravenly,
   as if planted next to the walls,—
   for only a princess has license
   to dance in the city streets: dance! . . .

DIE LIEBENDE

Ja ich sehne mich nach dir. Ich gleite
mich verlierend selbst mir aus der Hand,
ohne Hoffnung, daß ich Das bestreite,
was zu mir kommt wie aus deiner Seite
ernst und unbeirrt und unverwandt.

. . . jene Zeiten: O wie war ich Eines,
nichts was rief und nichts was mich verriet;
meine Stille war wie eines Steines,
über den der Bach sein Murmeln zieht.

Aber jetzt in diesen Frühlingswochen
hat mich etwas langsam abgebrochen
von dem unbewußten dunkeln Jahr.
Etwas hat mein armes warmes Leben
irgendeinem in die Hand gegeben,
der nicht weiß was ich noch gestern war.

WOMAN IN LOVE

Yes I long for you. I glide,
losing myself, out of my own hand,
without hope of conquering
what comes to me, as if out of your side,
grave and stark and undeterred.

. . . back then: O how complete I was,
nothing calling, nothing that divulged me;
my stillness was like a stone's
over which the brook makes its murmuring.

But now in these spring weeks
something has slowly broken me off
from the dark unconscious year.
Something has given my poor warm life
into the hand of someone random
who doesn't know what even yesterday I was.

DIE BRAUT

Ruf mich, Geliebter, ruf mich laut!
Laß deine Braut nicht so lange am Fenster stehn.
In den alten Platanenalleen
wacht der Abend nicht mehr:
sie sind leer.

Und kommst du mich nicht in das nächtliche Haus
mit deiner Stimme verschließen,
so muß ich mich aus meinen Händen hinaus
in die Gärten des Dunkelblaus
ergießen . . .

THE BRIDE

Call to me, love, call to me loudly!
Don't let your bride stand so long at the window.
In the old shaded plane-tree avenues
the evening no longer wakes:
they are empty.

And if you don't come and lock me up with your voice
in the deep nocturnal house,
then I must pour myself out of my hands
into the gardens of
dark blue . . .

DIE STILLE

Hörst du, Geliebte, ich hebe die Hände —
hörst du: es rauscht . . .
Welche Gebärde der Einsamen fände
sich nicht von vielen Dingen belauscht?
Hörst du, Geliebte, ich schließe die Lider,
und auch *das* ist Geräusch bis zu dir.
Hörst du, Geliebte, ich hebe sie wieder . . .
. . . aber warum bist du nicht hier.

Der Abdruck meiner kleinsten Bewegung
bleibt in der seidenen Stille sichtbar;
unvernichtbar drückt die geringste Erregung
in den gespannten Vorhang der Ferne sich ein.
Auf meinen Atemzügen heben und senken
die Sterne sich.
Zu meinen Lippen kommen die Düfte zur Tränke,
und ich erkenne die Handgelenke
entfernter Engel.
Nur die ich denke: Dich
seh ich nicht.

THE SILENCE

Listen, love, I lift my hands—
listen: there's a rustling . . .
What gesture of those all alone
might not be eavesdropped on by many things?
Listen, love, I close my eyes,
and even *that* makes sounds to reach you.
Listen, love, I open them . . .
. . . but why are you not here?

The imprint of my smallest motion
remains visible in the silken silence; .
indestructibly the least excitement
is stamped into the distance's taut curtain.
On my breathing the stars
rise and set.
At my lips fragrances come to drink,
and I recognize the wrists
of distant angels.
Only her of whom I think: You
I cannot see.

MUSIK

Was spielst du, Knabe? Durch die Gärten gings
wie viele Schritte, flüsternde Befehle.
Was spielst du, Knabe? Siehe deine Seele
verfing sich in den Stäben der Syrinx.

Was lockst du sie? Der Klang ist wie ein Kerker,
darin sie sich versäumt und sich versehnt;
stark ist dein Leben, doch dein Lied ist stärker,
an deine Sehnsucht schluchzend angelehnt. —

Gieb ihr ein Schweigen, daß die Seele leise
heimkehre in das Flutende und Viele,
darin sie lebte, wachsend, weit und weise,
eh du sie zwangst in deine zarten Spiele.

Wie sie schon matter mit den Flügeln schlägt:
so wirst du, Träumer, ihren Flug vergeuden,
daß ihre Schwinge, vom Gesang zersägt,
sie nicht mehr über meine Mauern trägt,
wenn ich sie rufen werde zu den Freuden.

MUSIC

What do you play, boy? It went through the gardens
like many footsteps, like whispering commands.
What do you play, boy? Look, your soul
got caught in the syrinx's bars.

Why do you lure it? The sound is like a prison
in which it languishes and pines away;
your life is strong, but your song is stronger,
sobbingly propped on your desire.—

Give it a silence, that the soul may lightly
turn home into the flooding and fullness
in which it lived, growing, wise and spacious,
until forced into your tender playing.

How it already beats its wings more faintly:
thus will you, dreamer, waste its flight,
so that its wings, severed by the singing,
will no longer carry it over my walls
when I shall call it to the deep delights.

DIE ENGEL

Sie haben alle müde Münde
und helle Seelen ohne Saum.
Und eine Sehnsucht (wie nach Sünde)
geht ihnen manchmal durch den Traum.

Fast gleichen sie einander alle;
in Gottes Gärten schweigen sie,
wie viele, viele Intervalle
in seiner Macht und Melodie.

Nur wenn sie ihre Flügel breiten,
sind sie die Wecker eines Winds:
als ginge Gott mit seinen weiten
Bildhauerhänden durch die Seiten
im dunklen Buch des Anbeginns.

THE ANGELS

They all have tired mouths
and bright seamless souls.
And a longing (as for sin)
sometimes haunts their dream.

They are almost all alike;
in God's gardens they keep still,
like many, many intervals
in his might and melody.

Only when they spread their wings
are they wakers of a wind:
as if God with his broad sculptor-
hands leafed through the pages
in the dark book of the beginning.

DER SCHUTZENGEL

Du bist der Vogel, dessen Flügel kamen,
wenn ich erwachte in der Nacht und rief.
Nur mit den Armen rief ich, denn dein Namen
ist wie ein Abgrund, tausend Nächte tief.
Du bist der Schatten, drin ich still entschlief,
und jeden Traum ersinnt in mir dein Samen, —
du bist das Bild, ich aber bin der Rahmen,
der dich ergänzt in glänzendem Relief.

Wie nenn ich dich? Sieh, meine Lippen lahmen.
Du bist der Anfang, der sich groß ergießt,
ich bin das langsame und bange Amen,
das deine Schönheit scheu beschließt.

Du hast mich oft aus dunklem Ruhn gerissen,
wenn mir das Schlafen wie ein Grab erschien
und wie Verlorengehen und Entfliehn, —
da hobst du mich aus Herzensfinsternissen
und wolltest mich auf allen Türmen hissen
wie Scharlachfahnen und wie Draperien.

Du: der von Wundern redet wie vom Wissen
und von den Menschen wie von Melodien
und von den Rosen: von Ereignissen,
die flammend sich in deinem Blick vollziehn, —
du Seliger, wann nennst du einmal Ihn,
aus dessen siebentem und letztem Tage
noch immer Glanz auf deinem Flügelschlage
verloren liegt . . .
Befiehlst du, daß ich frage?

THE GUARDIAN ANGEL

You are the bird whose wings came
when I wakened in the night and called.
Only with my arms I called, because your name
is like a chasm, a thousand nights deep.
You are the shadows in which I quietly slept,
and your seed devised in me each dream,—
you are the image, but I am the frame
that makes you stand in glittering relief.

What shall I call you? Look, my lips are lame.
You are the beginning that gushes forth,
I am the slow and fearful Amen
that timidly concludes your beauty.

You have often snatched me out of dark rest
when sleep seemed like a grave to me
and like getting lost and fleeing,—
then you raised me out of heart-darknesses
and tried to hoist me onto all towers
like scarlet flags and bunting.

You: who talk of miracles as of common knowledge
and of men and women as of melodies
and of roses: of events
that in your eyes blazingly take place,—
you blessed one, when will you at last name Him
from whose seventh and last day
shards of glory can still be found
on the beating of your wings . . .
Do I need to ask?

MARTYRINNEN

Martyrin ist sie. Und als harten Falls
mit einem Ruck
das Beil durch ihre kurze Jugend ging,
da legte sich der feine rote Ring
um ihren Hals, und war der erste Schmuck,
den sie mit einem fremden Lächeln nahm;
aber auch den erträgt sie nur mit Scham.
Und wenn sie schläft, muß ihre junge Schwester
(die, kindisch noch, sich mit der Wunde schmückt
von jenem Stein, der ihr die Stirn erdrückt)
die harten Arme um den Hals ihr halten,
und oft im Traume fleht die andre: Fester, fester.
Und da fällt es dem Kinde manchmal ein,
die Stirne mit dem Bild von jenem Stein
zu bergen in des sanften Nachtgewandes Falten,
das von der Schwester Atmen hell sich hebt,
voll wie ein Segel, das vom Winde lebt.

Das ist die Stunde, da sie heilig sind,
die stille Jungfrau und das blasse Kind.

Da sind sie wieder wie vor allem Leide
und schlafen arm und haben keinen Ruhm,
und ihre Seelen sind wie weiße Seide,
und von derselben Sehnsucht beben beide
und fürchten sich vor ihrem Heldentum.

Und du kannst meinen: wenn sie aus den Betten
aufstünden bei dem nächsten Morgenlichte
und, mit demselben träumenden Gesichte,
die Gassen kämen in den kleinen Städten, —
es bliebe keiner hinter ihnen staunen,
kein Fenster klirrte an den Häuserreihn,

MARTYRS

She is a martyr. And when crashing down
with a single jolt
the axe cut through her short youth,
the fine red ring drew itself
around her neck, and was the first jewelry,
which she accepted with a strange smile;
yet which she also only bashfully will bear.
And when she sleeps, her young sister
(who, still a child, is adorned with the wound
from that stone which crushed her brow)
has to hold her stiff arms around her neck,
and often in dream the other pleads: Tighter, tighter.
And then sometimes the child will think
to hide her brow with the image of that stone
in the folds of the fragile nightgown
that from her sister's breathing brightly rises,
full like a sail that lives on wind.

That is the hour when they are holy,
the silent virgin and the pale child.

Then they are again as before all suffering
and sleep deep sleep and have no glory
and their souls are as white silk,
and from the same longing both tremble
and are frightened by their heroism.

And you can think: when they'll arise
from their beds at the next light of dawn
and, with the same dreaming faces,
walk down the small cities' narrow streets,—
no one will stand behind them gawking,
no window will rattle on the housefronts,

und nirgends bei den Frauen ging ein Raunen,
und keines von den Kindern würde schrein.
Sie schritten durch die Stille in den Hemden
(die flachen Falten geben keinen Glanz)
so fremd, und dennoch keinem zum Befremden,
so wie zu Festen, aber ohne Kranz.

and nowhere will the women be whispering,
and none of the small children will shout.
They will step through the stillness in their shirts
(the shallow folds give off no shining)
so strange, and yet to no one's consternation,
as if to Easter, but with no wreath.

DIE HEILIGE

Das Volk war durstig; also ging das eine
durstlose Mädchen, ging die Steine
um Wasser flehen für ein ganzes Volk.
Doch ohne Zeichen blieb der Zweig der Weide,
und sie ermattete am langen Gehn
und dachte endlich nur, daß einer leide,
(ein kranker Knabe, und sie hatten beide
sich einmal abends ahnend angesehn).
Da neigte sich die junge Weidenrute
in ihren Händen dürstend wie ein Tier:
jetzt ging sie blühend über ihrem Blute,
und rauschend ging ihr Blut tief unter ihr.

THE SAINT

The nation was parched; and so the one
thirstless girl set out, walked to implore stones
to provide water for an entire race.
But the willow branch would give no sign,
and she grew exhausted from the long walking
and thought at last only that *one* suffered
(a sick boy, and once at evening each
had gazed at the other with foreboding).
Then the young willow rod bent down
in her hands thirsting like a wild beast:
now she went blossoming over her blood,
and her blood went rushing deep beneath her.

KINDHEIT

Da rinnt der Schule lange Angst und Zeit
mit Warten hin, mit lauter dumpfen Dingen.
O Einsamkeit, o schweres Zeitverbringen . . .
Und dann hinaus: die Straßen sprühn und klingen
und auf den Plätzen die Fontänen springen
und in den Gärten wird die Welt so weit —.
Und durch das alles gehn im kleinen Kleid,
ganz anders als die andern gehn und gingen —:
O wunderliche Zeit, o Zeitverbringen,
o Einsamkeit.

Und in das alles fern hinauszuschauen:
Männer und Frauen; Männer, Männer, Frauen
und Kinder, welche anders sind und bunt;
und da ein Haus und dann und wann ein Hund
und Schrecken lautlos wechselnd mit Vertrauen —:
O Trauer ohne Sinn, o Traum, o Grauen,
o Tiefe ohne Grund.

Und so zu spielen: Ball und Ring und Reifen
in einem Garten, welcher sanft verblaßt,
und manchmal die Erwachsenen zu streifen,
blind und verwildert in des Haschens Hast,
aber am Abend still, mit kleinen steifen
Schritten nachhaus zu gehn, fest angefaßt —:
O immer mehr entweichendes Begreifen,
o Angst, o Last.

Und stundenlang am großen grauen Teiche
mit einem kleinen Segelschiff zu knien;
es zu vergessen, weil noch andre, gleiche
und schönere Segel durch die Ringe ziehn,

CHILDHOOD

School's long anxiety and time slips past
with waiting, with endless dreary things.
O solitude, O heavy spending on and on of time . . .
And then outside: the streets flash and ring
and on the squares the fountains leap
and in the gardens all the world grows wide.—
And to go through it in one's small suit,
so unlike how the others go and used to go—:
O wondrous time, O spending on and on of time,
O solitude.

And to look far off into it all:
men and women; men, more men, women
and then children, who are different and bright;
and here a house and now and then a dog
and soundless terror changing back and forth with trust—:
O sadness without reason, O dream, O dread,
O depth without ground.

And so to play: ball and ring and hoops
in a garden that keeps softly fading,
and to brush sometimes against the grownups
blindly and wildly in the haste of tag,
but at evening quietly, with small stiff
steps to walk back home, your hand firmly held—:
O ever more escaping grasp of things,
O weight, O fear.

And for hours at the huge gray pond
to kneel entranced with a small sailboat;
to forget it, because yet other, similar
and more beautiful sails glide through the circles,

und denken müssen an das kleine bleiche
Gesicht, das sinkend aus dem Teiche schien —:
O Kindheit, o entgleitende Vergleiche.
Wohin? Wohin?

and to have to think about the small pale
face that sinking gazed out of the pond—:
O childhood, O likeness gliding off . . .
To where? To where?

AUS EINER KINDHEIT

Das Dunkeln war wie Reichtum in dem Raume,
darin der Knabe, sehr verheimlicht, saß.
Und als die Mutter eintrat wie im Traume,
erzitterte im stillen Schrank ein Glas.
Sie fühlte, wie das Zimmer sie verriet,
und küßte ihren Knaben: Bist du hier? . . .
Dann schauten beide bang nach dem Klavier,
denn manchen Abend hatte sie ein Lied,
darin das Kind sich seltsam tief verfing.

Es saß sehr still. Sein großes Schauen hing
an ihrer Hand, die ganz gebeugt vom Ringe,
als ob sie schwer in Schneewehn ginge,
über die weißen Tasten ging.

FROM A CHILDHOOD

The darkening was like treasures in the room
in which the boy, so deeply hidden, sat.
And when his mother entered as in a dream,
a glass trembled on the silent shelf.
She felt how the room was giving her away,
and kissed her boy: Are you here? . . .
Then both gazed fearfully toward the piano,
for many an evening she had a song
in which the child got strangely, deeply caught.

He sat stock still. His wide gaze hung
upon her hand, which, all weighed down by the ring,
as if it trudged through deep snowdrifts,
traveled over the white keys.

DER KNABE

Ich möchte einer werden so wie die,
die durch die Nacht mit wilden Pferden fahren,
mit Fackeln, die gleich aufgegangnen Haaren
in ihres Jagens großem Winde wehn.
Vorn möcht ich stehen wie in einem Kahne,
groß und wie eine Fahne aufgerollt.
Dunkel, aber mit einem Helm von Gold,
der unruhig glänzt. Und hinter mir gereiht
zehn Männer aus derselben Dunkelheit
mit Helmen, die, wie meiner, unstät sind,
bald klar wie Glas, bald dunkel, alt und blind.
Und einer steht bei mir und bläst uns Raum
mit der Trompete, welche blitzt und schreit,
und bläst uns eine schwarze Einsamkeit,
durch die wir rasen wie ein rascher Traum:
Die Häuser fallen hinter uns ins Knie,
die Gassen biegen sich uns schief entgegen,
die Plätze weichen aus: wir fassen sie,
und unsre Rosse rauschen wie ein Regen.

THE BOY

I want to become like one of those
who drive through the night with wild horses,
with torches, which like unloosened hair
blow in the great wind of their pursuit.
I want to stand in front as in a skiff,
huge and unfurled like a flag.
Dark, but with a helmet of gold that
gleams restlessly. And lined up behind me
ten men of that same darkness
with helmets that fret as mine does,
now clear as glass, now dark, old, and blind.
And one at my side blasts us space
with his trumpet, which flashes and screams out,
and blasts us a black solitude
through which we race like a rapid dream:
the houses fall to their knees behind us,
the streets slant against us,
the squares try to evade us: we seize them,
and our horses sweep down like rain.

DIE KONFIRMANDEN

(Paris, im Mai 1903)

In weißen Schleiern gehn die Konfirmanden
tief in das neue Grün der Gärten ein.
Sie haben ihre Kindheit überstanden,
und was jetzt kommt, wird anders sein.

O kommt es denn! Beginnt jetzt nicht die Pause,
das Warten auf den nächsten Stundenschlag?
Das Fest ist aus, und es wird laut im Hause,
und trauriger vergeht der Nachmittag . . .

Das war ein Aufstehn zu dem weißen Kleide
und dann durch Gassen ein geschmücktes Gehn
und eine Kirche, innen kühl wie Seide,
und lange Kerzen waren wie Alleen,
und alle Lichter schienen wie Geschmeide,
von feierlichen Augen angesehn.

Und es war still, als der Gesang begann:
Wie Wolken stieg er in der Wölbung an
und wurde hell im Niederfall; und linder
denn Regen fiel er in die weißen Kinder.
Und wie im Wind bewegte sich ihr Weiß,
und wurde leise bunt in seinen Falten
und schien verborgne Blumen zu enthalten —:
Blumen und Vögel, Sterne und Gestalten
aus einem alten fernen Sagenkreis.

Und draußen war ein Tag aus Blau und Grün
mit einem Ruf von Rot an hellen Stellen.
Der Teich entfernte sich in kleinen Wellen,
und mit dem Winde kam ein fernes Blühn
und sang von Gärten draußen vor der Stadt.

THE CONFIRMED

(Paris, May 1903)

In white veils the confirmed enter
deeply into the new green of the garden.
They have survived their childhood,
and what comes now will be something changed.

So let it come! Does not now the interim begin,
the wait for the next striking of the hour?
The festival is gone, and noises fill the house,
and more slowly the afternoon drags by . . .

That was an arising to the white gown
and then through streets an adorned walking
and a church, cool inside like silk,
and the long candles were like avenues,
and all lights glittered like jewelry
gazed at by festive eyes.

And it was silent when the chant began:
like clouds it rose inside the dome
and grew bright in its descent; and softer
than rain fell into the white children.
And their white fluttered as in the breeze,
and grew lightly colored in its folds
and seemed to hold hidden flowers—:
flowers and birds, stars and strange figures
from an old ring of stories, far away.

And outside was a day of blue and green
with a shout of red at bright places.
The pond kept retreating in small waves,
and with the wind came a distant flowering
and sang of gardens outside at the city's edge.

Es war, als ob die Dinge sich bekränzten,
sie standen licht, unendlich leicht besonnt;
ein Fühlen war in jeder Häuserfront,
und viele Fenster gingen auf und glänzten.

It was as if things wreathed themselves,
they stood brightly—infinitely light and calm;
a feeling was in every housefront,
and many windows opened up and shone.

DAS ABENDMAHL

Sie sind versammelt, staunende Verstörte,
um ihn, der wie ein Weiser sich beschließt
und der sich fortnimmt denen er gehörte
und der an ihnen fremd vorüberfließt.
Die alte Einsamkeit kommt über ihn,
die ihn erzog zu seinem tiefen Handeln;
nun wird er wieder durch den Ölwald wandeln,
und die ihn lieben werden vor ihm fliehn.

Er hat sie zu dem letzten Tisch entboten
und (wie ein Schuß die Vögel aus den Schoten
scheucht) scheucht er ihre Hände aus den Broten
mit seinem Wort: sie fliegen zu ihm her;
sie flattern bange durch die Tafelrunde
und suchen einen Ausgang. Aber *er*
ist überall wie eine Dämmerstunde.

THE LAST SUPPER

They are assembled—astonished, panicked—
around him, who like a sage concludes himself
and who withdraws from those he's gathered
and who ungraspably flows past them.
The old solitude comes over him,
which reared him for his deep action;
now he will wander through the olive woods again,
and those who love him will flee before him.

He has summoned them to the last meal
and (as a shot scatters birds from the wheat)
he scatters their hands from the loaves
with his word: they fly up to him;
they flap, terrified, all around the table
and seek a way out. But no use: *he*,
like a twilight hour, is everywhere.

The First Book, PART TWO

INITIALE

Aus unendlichen Sehnsüchten steigen
endliche Taten wie schwache Fontänen,
die sich zeitig und zitternd neigen.
Aber, die sich uns sonst verschweigen,
unsere frölichen Kräfte — zeigen
sich in diesen tanzenden Tränen.

INITIAL

Out of infinite desires rise
finite deeds like weak fountains
that fall back in early trembling arcs.
But those, which otherwise in us
keep hidden, our happy strengths—
they come forth in these dancing tears.

ZUM EINSCHLAFEN ZU SAGEN

Ich möchte jemanden einsingen,
bei jemandem sitzen und sein.
Ich möchte dich wiegen und kleinsingen
und begleiten schlafaus und schlafein.
Ich möchte der Einzige sein im Haus,
der wüßte: die Nacht war kalt.
Und möchte horchen herein und hinaus
in dich, in die Welt, in den Wald.
Die Uhren rufen sich schlagend an,
und man sieht der Zeit auf den Grund.
Und unten geht noch ein fremder Mann
und stört einen fremden Hund.
Dahinter wird Stille. Ich habe groß
die Augen auf dich gelegt;
und sie halten dich sanft und lassen dich los,
wenn ein Ding sich im Dunkel bewegt.

TO SAY BEFORE GOING TO SLEEP

I would like to sing someone to sleep,
to sit beside someone and be there.
I would like to rock you and sing softly
and go with you to and from sleep.
I would like to be the one in the house
who knew: The night was cold.
And I would like to listen in and listen out
into you, into the world, into the woods.
The clocks shout to one another striking,
and one sees to the bottom of time.
And down below one last, strange man walks by
and rouses a strange dog.
And after that comes silence.
I have laid my eyes upon you wide;
and they hold you gently and let you go
when something stirs in the dark.

MENSCHEN BEI NACHT

Die Nächte sind nicht für die Menge gemacht.
Von deinem Nachbar trennt dich die Nacht,
und du sollst ihn nicht suchen trotzdem.
Und machst du nachts deine Stube licht,
um Menschen zu schauen ins Angesicht,
so mußt du bedenken: wem.

Die Menschen sind furchtbar vom Licht entstellt,
das von ihren Gesichtern träuft,
und haben sie nachts sich zusammengesellt,
so schaust du eine wankende Welt
durcheinandergehäuft.
Auf ihren Stirnen hat gelber Schein
alle Gedanken verdrängt,
in ihren Blicken flackert der Wein,
an ihren Händen hängt
die schwere Gebärde, mit der sie sich
bei ihren Gesprächen verstehn;
und dabei sagen sie: *Ich* und *Ich*
und meinen: Irgendwen.

HUMAN BEINGS AT NIGHT

The nights are not made for the masses.
Night divides you from your neighbor,
and by no means are you to seek him out.
And if you light up your room at night
in order to look human beings in the face,
then you must ask yourself: whose.

Human beings are horribly warped by the light
that drips from their faces,
and if at night they have gathered together,
then you'll see a wavering world
all heaped up at random.
On their foreheads yellow glare has
driven out all thought,
in their eyes the wine flickers,
on their hands hangs
the heavy gesture with which they
understand one another in their talks;
and by which they say: *I* and *I*
and mean: Anybody.

DER NACHBAR

Fremde Geige, gehst du mir nach?
In wieviel fernen Städten schon sprach
deine einsame Nacht zu meiner?
Spielen dich hunderte? Spielt dich einer?

Giebt es in allen großen Städten
solche, die sich ohne dich
schon in den Flüssen verloren hätten?
Und warum trifft es immer mich?

Warum bin ich immer der Nachbar derer,
die dich bange zwingen zu singen
und zu sagen: Das Leben ist schwerer
als die Schwere von allen Dingen.

THE NEIGHBOR

Strange violin, do you follow me?
In how many distant cities before this
did your lonely night speak to mine?
Do hundreds play you? Does only one?

Are there in all of the great cities
those who without you would have
long since lost themselves in the rivers?
And why does it always reach me?

Why am I always the neighbor of those
who force you from fear to sing
and to say out loud: life is heavier
than the weight of all things.

PONT DU CARROUSEL

Der blinde Mann, der auf der Brücke steht,
grau wie ein Markstein namenloser Reiche,
er ist vielleicht das Ding, das immer gleiche,
um das von fern die Sternenstunde geht,
und der Gestirne stiller Mittelpunkt.
Denn alles um ihn irrt und rinnt und prunkt.

Er ist der unbewegliche Gerechte,
in viele wirre Wege hingestellt;
der dunkle Eingang in die Unterwelt
bei einem oberflächlichen Geschlechte.

PONT DU CARROUSEL

The blind man who stands on the bridge,
gray like a boundary stone of nameless kingdoms,
he is perhaps the thing, ever unchanging,
around which the far-off stellar hours move,
and the constellations' still midpoint.
For everything around him strays and struts and runs.

He is the immovable upright one
set down in many tangled paths;
the dark entrance to the underworld
amid a surface-dwelling race.

DER EINSAME

Wie einer, der auf fremden Meeren fuhr,
so bin ich bei den ewig Einheimischen;
die vollen Tage stehn auf ihren Tischen,
mir aber ist die Ferne voll Figur.

In mein Gesicht reicht eine Welt herein,
die vielleicht unbewohnt ist wie ein Mond,
sie aber lassen kein Gefühl allein,
und alle ihre Worte sind bewohnt.

Die Dinge, die ich weither mit mir nahm,
sehn selten aus, gehalten an das Ihre —:
in ihrer großen Heimat sind sie Tiere,
hier halten sie den Atem an vor Scham.

THE SOLITARY

Like one who's voyaged over foreign oceans
am I among these eternally at home;
the full days stand dumbly on their tables,
but to me the far-off is full of dream.

Deep inside my face a world reaches,
which perhaps is uninhabited like a moon;
but they leave no feeling to itself,
and all their words have long been lived in.

The things I brought with me from far away
appear outlandish, compared to theirs—:
in their great homeland they were wild animals,
here they hold their breath out of shame.

DIE ASCHANTI
(Jardin d'Acclimatation)

Keine Vision von fremden Ländern,
kein Gefühl von braunen Frauen, die
tanzen aus den fallenden Gewändern.

Keine wilde fremde Melodie.
Keine Lieder, die vom Blute stammten,
und kein Blut, das aus den Tiefen schrie.

Keine braunen Mädchen, die sich samten
breiteten in Tropenmüdigkeit;
keine Augen, die wie Waffen flammten,

und die Munde zum Gelächter breit.
Und ein wunderliches Sich-verstehen
mit der hellen Menschen Eitelkeit.

Und mir war so bange hinzusehen.

O wie sind die Tiere so viel treuer,
die in Gittern auf und niedergehn,
ohne Eintracht mit dem Treiben neuer
fremder Dinge, die sie nicht verstehn;
und sie brennen wie ein stilles Feuer
leise aus und sinken in sich ein,
teilnahmslos dem neuen Abenteuer
und mit ihrem großen Blut allein.

THE ASHANTI
(Jardin d'Acclimatation)

No vision of far-off countries,
no feeling of brown women who
dance out of their falling garments.

No wild unheard-of melodies.
No songs which issued from the blood,
and no blood which screamed out from the depths.

No brown girls who stretched out
velvetly in tropical exhaustion;
no eyes which blazed like weapons,

and the mouth broad with laughter.
And a bizarre agreement
with the light-skinned humans' vanity.

And it made me shudder seeing that.

O how much truer are the animals
that pace up and down in steel grids,
unrelated to the antics of the new
alien things which they don't understand;
and they burn like a silent fire
softly out and subside into themselves,
indifferent to the new adventure
and with their fierce instincts all alone.

DER LETZTE

Ich habe kein Vaterhaus,
und habe auch keines verloren;
meine Mutter hat mich in die Welt hinaus
geboren.
Da steh ich nun in der Welt und geh
in die Welt immer tiefer hinein,
und habe mein Glück und habe mein Weh
und habe jedes allein.
Und bin doch manch eines Erbe.
Mit drei Zweigen hat mein Geschlecht geblüht
auf sieben Schlössern im Wald,
und wurde seines Wappens müd
und war schon viel zu alt; —
und was sie mir ließen und was ich erwerbe
zum alten Besitze, ist heimatlos.
In meinen Händen, in meinem Schooß
muß ich es halten, bis ich sterbe.
Denn was ich fortstelle,
hinein in die Welt,
fällt,
ist wie auf eine Welle
gestellt.

THE LAST OF HIS LINE

I have no paternal house,
nor have I lost one;
my mother birthed me out
into the world.
Here I stand now in the world and go
ever deeper into the world
and have my happiness and have my woe
and have each one alone.
And yet to many a man am heir.
My family blossomed with three branches
on seven castles in the woods,
and grew weary of its coat of arms
and was already far too old;—
and what they left me and what I gained
of ancient ownership, is homeless.
In my hands, in my loins
I have to hold it all, until I die.
Since whatever I put away
out into the world
falls,
it is as if set down
upon a wave.

BANGNIS

Im welken Walde ist ein Vogelruf,
der sinnlos scheint in diesem welken Walde.
Und dennoch ruht der runde Vogelruf
in dieser Weile, die ihn schuf,
breit wie ein Himmel auf dem welken Walde.
Gefügig räumt sich alles in den Schrei:
Das ganze Land scheint lautlos drin zu liegen,
der große Wind scheint sich hineinzuschmiegen,
und die Minute, welche weiter will,
ist bleich und still, als ob sie Dinge wüßte,
an denen jeder sterben müßte,
aus ihm herausgestiegen.

APPREHENSION

In the faded forest there is a birdcall
which seems meaningless in this faded forest.
And yet the rounded birdcall rests
in this interim that shaped it,
wide as a sky upon the faded forest.
Pliantly everything makes room in the cry:
The whole land seems to lie in it soundlessly,
the great wind seems to nestle up inside,
and the moment, which wants to go on,
has, pale and silent, as if it knew things
for which anyone would have to die,
risen out of it.

KLAGE

O wie ist alles fern
und lange vergangen.
Ich glaube, der Stern,
von welchem ich Glanz empfange,
ist seit Jahrtausenden tot.
Ich glaube, im Boot,
das vorüberfuhr,
hörte ich etwas Banges sagen.
Im Hause hat eine Uhr
geschlagen . . .
In welchem Haus? . . .
Ich möchte aus meinem Herzen hinaus
unter den großen Himmel treten.
Ich möchte beten.
Und einer von allen Sternen
müßte wirklich noch sein.
Ich glaube, ich wüßte,
welcher allein
gedauert hat, —
welcher wie eine weiße Stadt
am Ende des Strahls in den Himmeln steht . . .

LAMENT

How everything is far away
and long deceased.
I think now, that the star
whose brightness reached me
has been dead for a thousand years.
I think now, that in the boat
which slipped past
I heard something fearful being said.
Inside the house a clock
just struck . . .
Inside what house? . . .
I would like to step out of my heart's door
and be under the great sky.
I would like to pray.
And surely one of all those stars
must still exist.
I think now, that I know
which one alone
has lasted,—
which one like a white city
stands at its light's end in the sky . . .

EINSAMKEIT

Die Einsamkeit ist wie ein Regen.
Sie steigt vom Meer den Abenden entgegen;
von Ebenen, die fern sind und entlegen,
geht sie zum Himmel, der sie immer hat.
Und erst vom Himmel fällt sie auf die Stadt.

Regnet hernieder in den Zwitterstunden,
wenn sich nach Morgen wenden alle Gassen
und wenn die Lieber, welche nichts gefunden,
enttäuscht und traurig von einander lassen;
und wenn die Menschen, die einander hassen,
in *einem* Bett zusammen schlafen müssen:

dann geht die Einsamkeit mit den Flüssen . . .

SOLITUDE

Solitude is like a rain.
It rises from the sea toward evening;
from plains, which are distant and remote,
it goes to the sky, which always has it.
And only then it falls from the sky on the city.

It rains down in the in-between hours,
when all the crooked streets turn toward morning,
and when the bodies, which found nothing,
leave each other feeling sad and disappointed;
and when the people, who hate each other,
have to sleep together in *one* bed:

then solitude flows with the rivers . . .

HERBSTTAG

Herr: es ist Zeit. Der Sommer war sehr groß.
Leg deinen Schatten auf die Sonnenuhren,
und auf den Fluren laß die Winde los.

Befiehl den letzten Früchten voll zu sein;
gieb ihnen noch zwei südlichere Tage,
dränge sie zur Vollendung hin und jage
die letzte Süße in den schweren Wein.

Wer jetzt kein Haus hat, baut sich keines mehr.
Wer jetzt allein ist, wird es lange bleiben,
wird wachen, lesen, lange Briefe schreiben
und wird in den Alleen hin und her
unruhig wandern, wenn die Blätter treiben.

AUTUMN DAY

Lord: it is time. The summer was immense.
Lay your shadows on the sundials,
and on the meadows let the winds go free.

Command the last fruits to be full;
give them just two more southern days,
urge them on to completion and chase
the last sweetness into the heavy wine.

Who has no house now, will never build one.
Who is alone now, will long remain so,
will stay awake, read, write long letters
and will wander restlessly up and down
the tree-lined streets, when the leaves are drifting.

ERINNERUNG

Und du wartest, erwartest das Eine,
das dein Leben unendlich vermehrt;
das Mächtige, Ungemeine,
das Erwachen der Steine,
Tiefen, dir zugekehrt.

Es dämmern im Bücherständer
die Bände in Gold und Braun;
und du denkst an durchfahrene Länder,
an Bilder, an die Gewänder
wiederverlorener Fraun.

Und da weißt du auf einmal: das war es.
Du erhebst dich, und vor dir steht
eines vergangenen Jahres
Angst und Gestalt und Gebet.

MEMORY

And you wait, await the one thing
that will infinitely increase your life;
the gigantic, the stupendous,
the awakening of stones,
depths turned round toward you.

The volumes in brown and gold
flicker dimly on the bookshelves;
and you think of lands traveled through,
of paintings, of the garments
of women found and lost.

And then all at once you know: that was it.
You rise, and there stands before you
the fear and prayer and shape
of a vanished year.

ENDE DES HERBSTES

Ich sehe seit einer Zeit,
wie alles sich verwandelt.
Etwas steht auf und handelt
und tötet und tut Leid.

Von Mal zu Mal sind all
die Gärten nicht dieselben;
von den gilbenden zu der gelben
langsamen Verfall:
wie war der Weg mir weit.

Jetzt bin ich bei den leeren
und schaue durch alle Alleen.
Fast bis zu den fernen Meeren
kann ich den ernsten schweren
verwehrenden Himmel sehn.

END OF AUTUMN

I have seen for some time
how everything is changing.
Something rises and acts
and kills and causes grief.

From one time to the next
all the gardens now are not the same;
from the yellowing to the
golden slow decay;
how long that path has been.

Now I stand amid emptiness
and gaze down all avenues.
Almost to the distant oceans
I can see the solemn ponderous
relentlessly denying sky.

HERBST

Die Blätter fallen, fallen wie von weit,
als welkten in den Himmeln ferne Gärten;
sie fallen mit verneinender Gebärde.

Und in den Nächten fällt die schwere Erde
aus allen Sternen in die Einsamkeit.

Wir alle fallen. Diese Hand da fällt.
Und sieh dir andre an: es ist in allen.

Und doch ist Einer, welcher dieses Fallen
unendlich sanft in seinen Händen hält.

AUTUMN

The leaves are falling, falling as if from far off,
as if in the heavens distant gardens withered;
they fall with gestures that say "no."

And in the nights the heavy earth falls
from all the stars into aloneness.

We are all falling. This hand is falling.
And look at the others: it is in them all.

And yet there is One who holds this falling
with infinite softness in his hands.

AM RANDE DER NACHT

Meine Stube und diese Weite,
wach über nachtendem Land, —
ist Eines. Ich bin eine Saite,
über rauschende breite
Resonanzen gespannt.

Die Dinge sind Geigenleiber,
von murrendem Dunkel voll;
drin träumt das Weinen der Weiber,
drin rührt sich im Schlafe der Groll
ganzer Geschlechter . . .
Ich soll
silbern erzittern: dann wird
Alles unter mir leben,
und was in den Dingen irrt,
wird nach dem Lichte streben,
das von meinem tanzenden Tone,
um welchen der Himmel wellt,
durch schmale, schmachtende Spalten
in die alten
Abgründe ohne
Ende fällt . . .

ON THE EDGE OF NIGHT

My room and this vastness,
awake over the darkening land,—
are one. I am a string,
stretched tightly over wide
raging resonances.

Things are violin-bodies
full of murmuring darkness:
in it dreams the weeping of women,
in it the grudge of whole
generations stirs in its sleep . . .
I shall vibrate
like silver; then everything
beneath me will live,
and whatever wanders lost in things
will strive toward the light
that from my dancing tone—
around which the heavens pulse—
through thin, pining rifts
into the old
abysses endlessly
falls . . .

GEBET

Nacht, stille Nacht, in die verwoben sind
ganz weiße Dinge, rote, bunte Dinge,
verstreute Farben, die erhoben sind
zu Einem Dunkel Einer Stille, — bringe
doch mich auch in Beziehung zu dem Vielen,
das du erwirbst und überredest. Spielen
denn meine Sinne noch zu sehr mit Licht?
Würde sich denn mein Angesicht
noch immer störend von den Gegenständen
abheben? Urteile nach meinen Händen:
Liegen sie nicht wie Werkzeug da und Ding?
Ist nicht der Ring selbst schlicht
an meiner Hand, und liegt das Licht
nicht ganz so, voll Vertrauen, über ihnen, —
als ob sie Wege wären, die, beschienen,
nicht anders sich verzweigen, als im Dunkel? . .

PRAYER

Night, still night, into which are woven
purely white things, red, brightly mottled things,
scattered colors, which are raised up
into One Darkness's One Stillness,—include me
also in the weft of that rich manifold
which you acquire and persuade. Do my senses
really still play too much with light?
Shall my face not forever stand out
as a disturbance in the world of
objects? Judge by my hands:
Do they not lie there like tool and thing?
Is not the ring itself simply
on my hand, and does not the light
lie exactly so, full of trust, over them,—
as if they were paths, which, brightly lit,
do not branch differently in darkness? . . .

FORTSCHRITT

Und wieder rauscht mein tiefes Leben lauter,
als ob es jetzt in breitern Ufern ginge.
Immer verwandter werden mir die Dinge
und alle Bilder immer angeschauter.
Dem Namenlosen fühl ich mich vertrauter:
Mit meinen Sinnen, wie mit Vögeln, reiche
ich in die windigen Himmel aus der Eiche,
und in den abgebrochnen Tag der Teiche
sinkt, wie auf Fischen stehend, mein Gefühl.

PROGRESS

And again my inmost life rushes louder,
as if it moved now between steeper banks.
Objects become ever more related to me,
and all pictures ever more perused.
I feel myself more trusting in the nameless:
with my senses, as with birds, I reach
into the windy heavens from the oak,
and into the small ponds' broken-off day
my feeling sinks, as if it stood on fishes.

VORGEFÜHL

Ich bin wie eine Fahne von Fernen umgeben.
Ich ahne die Winde, die kommen, und muß sie leben,
während die Dinge unten sich noch nicht rühren:
die Türen schließen noch sanft, und in den Kaminen ist Stille;
die Fenster zittern noch nicht, und der Staub ist noch schwer.

Da weiß ich die Stürme schon und bin erregt wie das Meer.
Und breite mich aus und falle in mich hinein
und werfe mich ab und bin ganz allein
in dem großen Sturm.

PRESENTIMENT

I am like a flag surrounded by distances.
I sense the winds that are coming, and must live them,
while the things down below don't yet stir:
the doors still close softly, and in the chimneys there's silence;
the windows don't tremble yet, and the dust is still calm.

Then I know the storms already and grow embroiled like the sea.
And spread myself out and plunge deep inside myself
and cast myself off and am entirely alone
in the great storm.

STURM

Wenn die Wolken, von Stürmen geschlagen,
jagen:
Himmel von hundert Tagen
über einem einzigen Tag —:

Dann fühl ich dich, Hetman, von fern
(der du deine Kosaken gern
zu dem größesten Herrn
führen wolltest).
Deinen waagrechten Nacken
fühl ich, Mazeppa.

Dann bin auch ich an das rasende Rennen
eines rauchenden Rückens gebunden;
alle Dinge sind mir verschwunden,
nur die Himmel kann ich erkennen:

Überdunkelt und überschienen
lieg ich flach unter ihnen,
wie Ebenen liegen;
meine Augen sind offen wie Teiche,
und in ihnen flüchtet das gleiche
Fliegen.

STORM

When the clouds, driven by storms,
stampede:
skies of a hundred daytimes
above a single day—:

Then I feel you, hetman, from afar
(you, who would gladly lead
your cossacks over
to the strongest lord).
Your neck level with the ground
I feel, Mazeppa.

Then I too am bound to the wild-eyed
racing of a smoking back;
all things have disappeared from me,
I can only recognize the sky:

Blanketed by darkness and bathed by light
I lie flat beneath it
the way plains lie;
my eyes are open like ponds,
and the same flying
flees in them . . .

ABEND IN SKÅNE

Der Park ist hoch. Und wie aus einem Haus
tret ich aus seiner Dämmerung heraus
in Ebene und Abend. In den Wind,
denselben Wind, den auch die Wolken fühlen,
die hellen Flüsse und die Flügelmühlen,
die langsam mahlend stehn am Himmelsrand.
Jetzt bin auch ich ein Ding in seiner Hand,
das kleinste unter diesen Himmeln. —Schau:

Ist das Ein Himmel?:
               Selig lichtes Blau,
in das sich immer reinere Wolken drängen,
und drunter alle Weiß in Übergängen,
und drüber jenes dünne, große Grau,
warmwallend wie auf roter Untermalung,
und über allem diese stille Strahlung
sinkender Sonne.

               Wunderlicher Bau,
in sich bewegt und von sich selbst gehalten,
Gestalten bildend, Riesenflügel, Falten
und Hochgebirge vor den ersten Sternen
und plötzlich, da: ein Tor in solche Fernen,
wie sie vielleicht nur Vögel kennen . . .

EVENING IN SKÅNE

The park is high. And as out of a house
I step out of its glimmering half-light
into openness and evening. Into the wind,
the same wind that the clouds feel,
the bright rivers and the turning mills
that stand slowly grinding at the sky's edge.
Now I too am a thing held in its hand,
the smallest thing under this sky. —Look:

Is *that* one sky?:
                    Blissfully lucid blue,
into which ever purer clouds throng,
and under it all white in endless changes,
and over it that huge, thin-spun gray,
pulsing warmly as on red underpaint,
and over everything this silent radiance
of a setting sun.

                    Miraculous structure,
moved within itself and upheld by itself,
shaping figures, giant wings, faults
and high mountain ridges before the first star
and suddenly, there: a gate into such
distances as perhaps only birds know . . .

ABEND

Der Abend wechselt langsam die Gewänder,
die ihm ein Rand von alten Bäumen hält;
du schaust: und von dir scheiden sich die Länder,
ein himmelfahrendes und eins, das fällt;

und lassen dich, zu keinem ganz gehörend,
nicht ganz so dunkel wie das Haus, das schweigt,
nicht ganz so sicher Ewiges beschwörend
wie das, was Stern wird jede Nacht und steigt —

und lassen dir (unsäglich zu entwirrn)
dein Leben bang und riesenhaft und reifend,
so daß es, bald begrenzt und bald begreifend,
abwechselnd Stein in dir wird und Gestirn.

EVENING

Slowly the evening puts on the garments
held for it by a rim of ancient trees;
you watch: and the lands divide from you,
one going heavenward, one that falls;

and leave you, to neither quite belonging,
not quite so dark as the house sunk in silence,
not quite so surely pledging the eternal
as that which grows star each night and climbs—

and leave you (inexpressibly to untangle)
your life afraid and huge and ripening,
so that it, now bound in and now embracing,
grows alternately stone in you and star.

ERNSTE STUNDE

Wer jetzt weint irgendwo in der Welt,
   ohne Grund weint in der Welt,
   weint über mich.

Wer jetzt lacht irgendwo in der Nacht,
   ohne Grund lacht in der Nacht,
   lacht mich aus.

Wer jetzt geht irgendwo in der Welt,
   ohne Grund geht in der Welt,
   geht zu mir.

Wer jetzt stirbt irgendwo in der Welt,
   ohne Grund stirbt in der Welt:
   sieht mich an.

SOLEMN HOUR

Whoever weeps now anywhere out in the world,
   weeps without cause in the world,
   weeps for me.

Whoever laughs now anywhere out in the world,
   laughs without cause in the world,
   laughs at me.

Whoever walks now anywhere out in the world,
   walks without cause in the world,
   walks toward me.

Whoever dies now anywhere out in the world,
   dies without cause in the world:
   looks at me.

STROPHEN

Ist einer, der nimmt alle in die Hand,
daß sie wie Sand durch seine Finger rinnen.
Er wählt die schönsten aus den Königinnen
und läßt sie sich in weißen Marmor hauen,
still liegend in des Mantels Melodie;
und legt die Könige zu ihren Frauen,
gebildet aus dem gleichen Stein wie sie.

Ist einer, der nimmt alle in die Hand,
daß sie wie schlechte Klingen sind und brechen.
Er ist kein Fremder, denn er wohnt im Blut,
das unser Leben ist und rauscht und ruht.
Ich kann nicht glauben, daß er Unrecht tut;
doch hör ich viele Böses von ihm sprechen.

STROPHES

There's one who takes all people in his hand,
so that like silt they trickle through his fingers.
He picks out the loveliest of the queens
and has them carved for him in white marble,
lying quietly in their mantle's song;
and places the kings down beside their wives,
fashioned from the same stone as they.

There's one who takes all people in his hand,
so that they are like bad blades and break.
He is no stranger, for he dwells in the blood
that is our life and rushes on and rests.
I cannot think he acts unjustly;
yet I hear many speaking evil of him.

The Second Book, PART ONE

INITIALE

Gieb deine Schönheit immer hin
ohne Rechnen und Reden.
Du schweigst. Sie sagt für dich: Ich bin.
Und kommt in tausendfachem Sinn,
kommt endlich über jeden.

INITIAL

Let your beauty manifest itself
without talking and calculation.
You are silent. It says for you: I am.
And comes in meaning thousandfold,
comes at long last over everyone.

VERKÜNDIGUNG
Die Worte des Engels

Du bist nicht näher an Gott als wir;
wir sind ihm alle weit.
Aber wunderbar sind dir
die Hände benedeit.
So reifen sie bei keiner Frau,
so schimmernd aus dem Saum:
ich bin der Tag, ich bin der Tau,
du aber bist der Baum.

Ich bin jetzt matt, mein Weg war weit,
vergieb mir, ich vergaß,
was Er, der groß in Goldgeschmeid
wie in der Sonne saß,
dir künden ließ, du Sinnende,
(verwirrt hat mich der Raum).
Sieh: ich bin das Beginnende,
du aber bist der Baum.

Ich spannte meine Schwingen aus
und wurde seltsam weit;
jetzt überfließt dein kleines Haus
von meinem großen Kleid.
Und dennoch bist du so allein
wie nie und schaust mich kaum;
das macht: ich bin ein Hauch im Hain,
du aber bist der Baum.

Die Engel alle bangen so,
lassen einander los:
noch nie war das Verlangen so,
so ungewiß und groß.
Vielleicht, daß Etwas bald geschieht,

ANNUNCIATION
The Words of the Angel

You are not nearer God than we;
we are all far from him.
And yet how beautifully
your hands are blessed.
No woman's ripen that way,
shimmering thus out of the sleeve:
I am the day, I am the dew,
you though are the tree.

I'm exhausted now, my way was far,
forgive me, I've forgotten
what He, who great in gold array
sat throned as in the sun,
gave me to tell you, you pensive one,
(space has me confused).
Look: I'm whatever is beginning,
you though are the tree.

I stretched my wings to rest them
and grew oddly vast;
now your small house overflows
with my great brocade.
And yet you are more alone
than ever and scarcely notice me;
it's true: I am a breath inside the forest,
you though are the tree.

The angels all grow afraid,
let one another go:
never was desire like this,
so vague and great.
Perhaps something soon will happen

das du im Traum begreifst.
Gegrüßt sei, meine Seele sieht:
du bist bereit und reifst.
Du bist ein großes, hohes Tor,
und aufgehn wirst du bald.
Du, meines Liedes liebstes Ohr,
jetzt fühle ich: mein Wort verlor
sich in dir wie im Wald.

So kam ich und vollendete
dir tausendeinen Traum.
Gott sah mich an; er blendete . . .

Du aber bist der Baum.

that you now grasp in dream.
Greetings to you, my soul now sees:
you are ready and grow ripe.
You are a great, high shining gate,
and you will open soon.
You, my song's most cherished ear,
now I feel: my word got lost
in you as in a wood.

And so I came that way and made complete
your thousand and one dreams.
God looked at me: the light was blinding . . .

You though are the tree.

DIE HEILIGEN DREI KÖNIGE

Legende

Einst als am Saum der Wüsten sich
auftat die Hand des Herrn
wie eine Frucht, die sommerlich
verkündet ihren Kern,
da war ein Wunder: Fern
erkannten und begrüßten sich
drei Könige und ein Stern.

Drei Könige von Unterwegs
und der Stern Überall,
die zogen alle (überlegs!)
so rechts ein Rex und links ein Rex
zu einem stillen Stall.

Was brachten die nicht alles mit
zum Stall von Bethlehem!
Weithin erklirrte jeder Schritt,
und der auf einem Rappen ritt,
saß samten und bequem.
Und der zu seiner Rechten ging,
der war ein goldner Mann,
und der zu seiner Linken fing
mit Schwung und Schwing
und Klang und Kling
aus einem runden Silberding,
das wiegend und in Ringen hing,
ganz blau zu rauchen an.
Da lachte der Stern Überall
so seltsam über sie,
und lief voraus und stand am Stall
und sagte zu Marie:

THE THREE HOLY KINGS
Legend

Once long ago when at the desert's edge
the Lord's hand spread open—
as if a fruit should deep in summer
proclaim its seed—
there was a miracle: across
vast distances a constellation formed
out of three kings and a star.

Three kings from On-the-Way
and the star Everywhere,
who all pushed on (just think!)
to the right a Rex and the left a Rex
toward a silent stall.

What was there that they *didn't* bring
to that stall of Bethlehem!
Each step clanked out ahead of them,
and he who rode the sable horse
sat plush and velvet-snug.
And he who walked upon his right
was like some man of gold,
and he who sauntered on his left
with sling and swing
and jang and jing
from a round silver thing
that hung swaying inside rings,
began to smoke deep blue.
Then the star Everywhere laughed
so strangely at them,
and ran ahead and found the stall
and said to Mary:

Da bring ich eine Wanderschaft
aus vieler Fremde her.
Drei Könige mit Magenkraft,
von Gold und Topas schwer
und dunkel, tumb und heidenhaft, —
erschrick mir nicht zu sehr.
Sie haben alle drei zuhaus
zwölf Töchter, keinen Sohn,
so bitten sie sich deinen aus
als Sonne ihres Himmelblaus
und Trost für ihren Thron.
Doch mußt du nicht gleich glauben: bloß
ein Funkelfürst und Heidenscheich
sei deines Sohnes Los.
Bedenk, der Weg ist groß.
Sie wandern lange, Hirten gleich,
inzwischen fällt ihr reifes Reich
weiß Gott wem in den Schooß.
Und während hier, wie Westwind warm,
der Ochs ihr Ohr umschnaubt,
sind sie vielleicht schon alle arm
und so wie ohne Haupt.
Drum mach mit deinem Lächeln licht
die Wirrnis, die sie sind,
und wende du dein Angesicht
nach Aufgang und dein Kind;
dort liegt in blauen Linien,
was jeder dir verließ:
Smaragda und Rubinien
und die Tale von Türkis.

I am bringing here an errantry
made up of many strangers.
Three kings with ancient might
heavy with gold and topaz
and dark, dim, and heathenish,—
but don't you be afraid.
They have all three at home
twelve daughters, not one son,
so they'll ask for use of yours
as sunshine for their heaven's blue
and comfort for their throne.
Yet don't straightaway believe: simply
some sparkle-prince and heathen-sheik
should be your young son's lot.
Consider: the road is long.
They've wandered far, like herdsmen,
while back home their ripe empire falls
into the lap of God knows whom.
And while here, warmly like westwind,
the ox snorts into their ear,
back there they may already be bereft
and headless, for all they know.
So with your smile cast light
on that confusion which they are,
and turn your countenance
toward dawning with your child:
there in blue lines lies
what each one left for you:
Emeralda and Rubinien
and the Valley of Turquoise.

IN DER CERTOSA

Ein jeder aus der weißen Bruderschaft
vertraut sich pflanzend seinem kleinen Garten.
Auf jedem Beete steht, wer jeder sei.
Und Einer harrt in heimlichen Hoffahrten,
daß ihm im Mai
die ungestümen Blüten offenbarten
ein Bild von seiner unterdrückten Kraft.

Und seine Hände halten, wie erschlafft,
sein braunes Haupt, das schwer ist von den Säften,
die ungeduldig durch das Dunkel rollen,
und sein Gewand, das faltig, voll und wollen,
zu seinen Füßen fließt, ist stramm gestrafft
um seinen Armen, die, gleich starken Schäften,
die Hände tragen, welche träumen sollen.

Kein Miserere und kein Kyrie
will seine junge, runde Stimme ziehn,
vor keinem Fluche will sie fliehn:
sie ist kein Reh.
Sie ist ein Roß und bäumt sich im Gebiß,
und über Hürde, Hang und Hindernis
will sie ihn tragen, weit und weggewiß,
ganz ohne Sattel will sie tragen ihn.

Er aber sitzt, und unter den Gedanken
zerbrechen fast die breiten Handgelenke,
so schwer wird ihm der Sinn und immer schwerer.

Der Abend kommt, der sanfte Wiederkehrer,
ein Wind beginnt, die Wege werden leerer,
und Schatten sammeln sich im Talgesenke.

IN THE CERTOSA

Each member of the white brotherhood
guilelessly plants his devout little garden.
On each bed it states who each one is.
And one of them waits in secret isolation,
knowing that in May
the impetuous bloomings will be for him
an image of his stifled strengths.

And his hands hold, as if grown tired,
his brown head, which is heavy from the force
that rolls impatiently through the dark,
and his robe, which in folds, full and woolen,
flows to his feet, is stretched taut
around his arms, which, like strong shafts,
bear the hands supposed to dream.

No Miserere and no Kyrie
will his young, round voice draw out,
before no curse will it flee;
it is no doe.
It is a horse and rears against the bit,
and over hurdle, cliff, and hindrance
it will bear him, far and certain of the path—
even without saddle it will bear him.

But he sits, and beneath his thoughts
his broad wrists almost break,
as his mind grows heavier, always heavier.

The evening comes, returning softly,
a wind starts up, the paths grow emptier,
and shadows gather in the valley's cup.

Und wie ein Kahn, der an der Kette schwankt,
so wird der Garten ungewiß und hangt
wie windgewiegt auf lauter Dämmerung.
Wer löst ihn los? . . .

Der Frate ist so jung,
und langelang ist seine Mutter tot.
Er weiß von ihr: sie nannten sie *La Stanca*;
sie war ein Glas, ganz zart und klar. Man bot
es einem, der es nach dem Trunk zerschlug
wie einen Krug.

So ist der Vater.
Und er hat sein Brot
als Meister in den roten Marmorbrüchen.
Und jede Wöchnerin in Pietrabianca
hat Furcht, daß er des Nachts mit seinen Flüchen
vorbei an ihrem Fenster kommt und droht.

Sein Sohn, den er der Donna Dolorosa
geweiht in einer Stunde wilder Not,
sinnt im Arkadenhofe der Certosa,
sinnt, wie umrauscht von rötlichen Gerüchen:
denn seine Blumen blühen alle rot.

And like a boat that sways upon its chain,
the garden grows indistinct and hangs
as though wind-cradled on sheer twilight.
Who will set it free? . . .

The Frate is so young,
and his mother has been dead for ages.
he knows about her; they called her *La Stanca*;
she was a glass, all delicate and clear. It was given
to one who, after drinking, smashed it
like a jug.

That is the father.
And he makes his living
as foreman in the red marble quarries.
And every woman lying-in in Pietrabianca
dreads him, since at night with his mad curses
he may pass by her window, boding ill.

His son, whom to the Donna Dolorosa
he dedicated in an hour of wild distress,
broods in the arcaded courtyard of the Certosa,
broods, as in a swirl of reddish smells:
for his flowers all bloom red.

DAS JÜNGSTE GERICHT
Aus den Blättern eines Mönchs

Sie werden Alle wie aus einem Bade
aus ihren mürben Grüften auferstehn;
denn alle glauben an das Wiedersehn,
und furchtbar ist ihr Glauben, ohne Gnade.

Sprich leise, Gott! Es könnte einer meinen,
daß die Posaune deiner Reiche rief;
und ihrem Ton ist keine Tiefe tief:
da steigen alle Zeiten aus den Steinen,
und alle die Verschollenen erscheinen
in welken Leinen, brüchigen Gebeinen
und von der Schwere ihrer Schollen schief.
Das wird ein wunderliches Wiederkehren
in eine wunderliche Heimat sein;
auch die dich niemals kannten, werden schrein
und deine Größe wie ein Recht begehren:
wie Brot und Wein.

Allschauender, du kennst das wilde Bild,
das ich in meinem Dunkel zitternd dichte.
Durch dich kommt Alles, denn du bist das Tor, —
und Alles war in deinem Angesichte,
eh es in unserm sich verlor.
Du kennst das Bild vom riesigen Gerichte:

Ein Morgen ist es, doch aus einem Lichte,
das deine reife Liebe nie erschuf,
ein Rauschen ist es, nicht aus deinem Ruf,
ein Zittern, nicht von göttlichem Verzichte,
ein Schwanken, nicht in deinem Gleichgewichte.
Ein Rascheln ist und ein Zusammenraffen
in allen den geborstenen Gebäuden,

THE LAST JUDGMENT
From the Pages of a Monk

They will all as if out of a bath
out of their moldering graves resurrect;
for they all believe in the reunion,
and their belief is terrible, without grace.

Speak softly, God! It could mean to someone
that the trumpets of your kingdom called;
and for their sound no depth is deep enough:
then all times rise out of the stones,
and all the long-lost appear
in faded linen, brittle skeletons
and crooked from the weight of their clods.
That will be a miraculous return
into a wondrous homeland;
even those who never knew you will scream
and crave your greatness like a right:
like bread and wine.

All-seeing one, you know that wild picture
that in my darkness I tremblingly compose.
Through you comes everything, for you are the gate,—
and everything was in your countenance
before it lost itself in ours.
You know that picture of the huge judgment:

There is a morning, yet of a light
that your mature love never could create,
there is a sound, not from your call,
a trembling, not from divine relinquishment,
a swaying, not in your equipoise.
There is a rustling and a mustering up
in all of the exploded structures,

ein Sichentgelten und ein Sichvergeuden,
ein Sichbegatten und ein Sichbegaffen,
und ein Betasten aller alten Freuden
und aller Lüste welke Wiederkehr.
Und über Kirchen, die wie Wunden klaffen,
ziehn schwarze Vögel, die du nie erschaffen,
in irren Zügen hin und her.

So ringen sie, die lange Ausgeruhten,
und packen sich mit ihren nackten Zähnen
und werden bange, weil sie nicht mehr bluten,
und suchen, wo die Augenbecher gähnen,
mit kalten Fingern nach den toten Tränen.
Und werden müde. Wenige Minuten
nach ihrem Morgen bricht ihr Abend ein.
Sie werden ernst und lassen sich allein
und sind bereit, im Sturme aufzusteigen,
wenn sich auf deiner Liebe heitrem Wein
die dunklen Tropfen deines Zornes zeigen,
um deinem Urteil nah zu sein.
Und da beginnt es, nach dem großen Schrein:
das übergroße fürchterliche Schweigen.

Sie sitzen alle wie vor schwarzen Türen
in einem Licht, das sie, wie mit Geschwüren,
mit vielen grellen Flecken übersät.
Und wachsend wird der Abend alt und spät.
Und Nächte fallen dann in großen Stücken
auf ihre Hände und auf ihren Rücken,
der wankend sich mit schwarzer Last belädt.
Sie warten lange. Ihre Schultern schwanken
unter dem Drucke wie ein dunkles Meer,
sie sitzen, wie versunken in Gedanken,
und sind doch leer.
Was stützen sie die Stirnen?
Ihre Gehirne denken irgendwo

a self-repaying and a self-squandering,
a self-mating and a self-gaping-at,
and a palpating of all old joys
and of all pleasures' pale return.
And over churches, torn open like wounds,
dark birds you never made
steer endlessly in crazed formations.

Thus they wrestle, the long-recuperated,
and seize each other with their naked teeth
and grow afraid, because they bleed no longer,
and grope, where the eyes' beakers gape,
with cold fingers for the dead tears.
And grow tired. A few minutes
after their morning their evening comes.
They grow solemn and self-absorbed
and are prepared to rise up in the storm
when on your love's bright wine
the dark drops of your anger will appear,
so they will be near your judgment.
And then it begins, after the great screaming:
the overwhelming terrifying silence.

They all sit as if before black gates
in a light which, as if with bleeding sores,
studs them with many iridescent flecks.
And the evening, waxing, becomes old and late.
And night falls then in huge pieces
down upon their hands and on their necks,
which, wavering, load themselves with black weight.
They remain in place. Their shoulders sway
beneath the pressure like a dark sea,
they sit, as if deep in thought,
and yet are empty.
Why do they prop their brows?
Their brains think somewhere

tief in der Erde, eingefallen, faltig:
Die ganze alte Erde denkt gewaltig,
und ihre großen Bäume rauschen so.

Allschauender, gedenkst du dieses bleichen
und bangen Bildes, das nicht seinesgleichen
unter den Bildern deines Willens hat?
Hast du nicht Angst vor dieser stummen Stadt,
die, an dir hangend wie ein welkes Blatt,
sich heben will zu deines Zornes Zeichen?
O, greife allen Tagen in die Speichen,
daß sie zu bald nicht diesem Ende nahen, —
vielleicht gelingt es dir noch auszuweichen
dem großen Schweigen, das wir beide sahen.
Vielleicht kannst du noch einen aus uns heben,
der diesem fürchterlichen Wiederleben
den Sinn, die Sehnsucht und die Seele nimmt,
einen, der bis in seinen Grund ergrimmt
und dennoch froh, durch alle Dinge schwimmt,
der Kräfte unbekümmerter Verbraucher,
der sich auf allen Saiten geigt
und unversehrt als unerkannter Taucher
in alle Tode niedersteigt.
. . . Oder, wie hoffst du diesen Tag zu tragen,
der länger ist als aller Tage Längen,
mit seines Schweigens schrecklichen Gesängen,
wenn dann die Engel dich, wie lauter Fragen,
mit ihrem schauerlichen Flügelschlagen
umdrängen?
Sieh, wie sie zitternd in den Schwingen hängen
und dir mit hunderttausend Augen klagen,
und ihres sanften Liedes Stimmen wagen
sich aus den vielen wirren Übergängen
nicht mehr zu heben zu den klaren Klängen.
Und wenn die Greise mit den breiten Bärten,
die dich berieten bei den besten Siegen,

deep in the earth, collapsed, in folds:
the entire ancient earth thinks prodigiously,
and the murmur of its great trees grows.

All-seeing one, do you recall this
pale and fearful picture, which has no like
among the many pictures of your will?
Are you not frightened by this mute city,
which, clinging to you like a withered leaf,
wants to rise up as your anger's sign?
O, set yourself against the wheeling of all days
to slow their progress toward this end,—
perhaps you can still manage to avert
that great silence which we both have seen.
Perhaps you can still raise one from us
who extracts from this dread reanimation
the meaning, the desire, and the soul,
one who, enraged with all his heart
and yet serene, swims through all things,
the powers' nonchalant consumer,
who plays himself on all strings
and who unharmed, like secret divers,
down into all deaths descends.
. . . If not, how do you hope to bear this day—
which is longer than all days' durations
with its silence's terrifying hymns,
when the angels, like endless questions,
with their eerie fluttering
crowd around you?
Look how they hang trembling in the air
and lament to you with a hundred thousand faces,
and no longer dare to lift their soft song's voice
out of the many confused transitions
into the lucid tones.
And if the old broad-bearded sages
who gave you counsel in your best victories

nur leise ihre weißen Häupter wiegen,
und wenn die Frauen, die den Sohn dir nährten,
und die von ihm Verführten, die Gefährten,
und alle Jungfraun, die sich ihm gewährten:
die lichten Birken deiner dunklen Gärten, —
wer soll dir helfen, wenn sie alle schwiegen?

Und nur dein Sohn erhübe sich unter denen,
welche sitzen um deinen Thron.
Grübe sich deine Stimme dann in sein Herz?
Sagte dein einsamer Schmerz dann:
Sohn!
Suchtest du dann das Angesicht
dessen, der das Gericht gerufen,
dein Gericht und deinen Thron:
Sohn!
Hießest du, Vater, dann deinen Erben,
leise begleitet von Magdalenen,
niedersteigen zu jenen,
die sich sehnen, wieder zu sterben?

Das wäre dein letzter Königserlaß,
die letzte Huld und der letzte Haß.
Aber dann käme Alles zu Ruh:
der Himmel und das Gericht und du.
Alle Gewänder des Rätsels der Welt,
das sich so lange verschleiert hält,
fallen mit dieser Spange.
. . . Doch mir ist bange . . .

Allschauender, sieh, wie mir bange ist,
miß meine Qual!
Mir ist bange, daß du schon lange vergangen bist.
Als du zum erstenmal
in deinem Alleserfassen
das Bild dieses blassen

only limply sway their grizzled heads,
and if those women who nursed your son for you,
and those enticed by him, his companions,
and all virgins who pledged themselves to him,
the bright birch trees in your dark gardens,—
who shall help you, if they all are silent?

And only your son would arise among those
who sit mutely around your throne.
Would your voice engrave itself then in his heart?
Would your solitary pain say then:
Son!
Would you search then for the face
of the one who has called the judgment,
your judgment and your throne:
Son!
Would you then, Father, bid your heir,
gently accompanied by Magdalene,
to descend to those
who desire to die again?
That would be your last royal edict,
the last favor and the last hate.
But then everything would come to rest:
the heavens and the judgment and you.
All the garments of the riddle of the world,
which has for so long kept itself veiled,
fall with this clasp.
. . . Yet I am afraid . . .

All-seeing one, look how afraid I am,
gauge my anguish!
I am afraid that you have long since vanished.
When for the first time
with your great grasp of things
you saw the image

Gerichtes sahst,
dem du dich hülflos nahst, Allschauender.
Bist du damals entflohn?
Wohin?
Vertrauender
kann keiner dir kommen
als ich,
der ich dich
nicht um Lohn
verraten will wie alle die Frommen.
Ich will nur, weil ich verborgen bin
und müde wie du, noch müder vielleicht,
und weil meine Angst vor dem großen Gericht
deiner gleicht,
will ich mich dicht,
Gesicht bei Gesicht,
an dich heften;
mit einigen Kräften
werden wir wehren dem großen Rade,
über welches die mächtigen Wasser gehn,
die rauschen und schnauben —
denn: wehe, sie werden auferstehn.
So ist ihr Glauben: groß und ohne Gnade.

of this pale judgment
toward which you helplessly draw near, all-seeing one.
Did you abscond back then?
To where?
No one can approach you
more trustfully
than I,
for I don't wish
to betray you for reward
like all the pious.
I want only, since I am hidden
and weary like you, even wearier perhaps,
and since my fear confronted with the great judgment
is like your own,
I want to join with you,
face next to face,
at your side;
with united strengths
we will stem the great wheel
over which the powerful waters run,
roaring and spewing—
then: alas, they will resurrect.
Such is their belief: great and without grace.

KARL DER ZWÖLFTE VON SCHWEDEN
REITET IN DER UKRAINE

Könige in Legenden
sind wie Berge im Abend. Blenden
jeden, zu dem sie sich wenden.
Die Gürtel um ihre Lenden
und die lastenden Mantelenden
sind Länder und Leben wert.
Mit den reichgekleideten Händen
geht, schlank und nackt, das Schwert.

•

Ein junger König aus Norden war
in der Ukraine geschlagen.
Der haßte Frühling und Frauenhaar
und die Harfen und was sie sagen.
Der ritt auf einem grauen Pferd,
sein Auge schaute grau
und hatte niemals Glanz begehrt
zu Füßen einer Frau.
Keine war seinem Blicke blond,
keine hat küssen ihn gekonnt;
und wenn er zornig war,
so riß er einen Perlenmond
aus wunderschönem Haar.
Und wenn ihn Trauer überkam,
so machte er ein Mädchen zahm
und forschte, wessen Ring sie nahm
und wem sie ihren bot —
und: hetzte ihr den Bräutigam
mit hundert Hunden tot.

Und er verließ sein graues Land,
das ohne Stimme war,

CHARLES THE TWELFTH OF SWEDEN
RIDES IN THE UKRAINE

Kings in legends are like
mountains at evening. Dazzle
those to whom they turn.
The belt that girds their loins
and the burdensome mantle
have cost countries and lives.
With the richly gloved hands
goes, slender and naked, the sword.

•

A young king from the North
was beaten in the Ukraine.
He hated springtime and golden hair
and harps and what they say.
He rode on a gray horse,
his eyes gazed grayly
and had never dreamed of glory
at any woman's feet.
None was to his eyes fair,
none had ever won from him a kiss;
and when he grew furious
he ripped a crescent-shaped tiara
out of the softest hair.
And when a sadness overcame him
he forced a young girl's will
and found out whose ring she'd taken
and to whom she'd offered hers—
and: hounded her betrothed to death
with a hundred hunting-dogs.

And he left his gray country,
which was devoid of voice,

und ritt in einen Widerstand
und kämpfte um Gefahr,
bis ihn das Wunder überwand:
wie träumend ging ihm seine Hand
von Eisenband zu Eisenband
und war kein Schwert darin;
er war zum Schauen aufgewacht:
es schmeichelte die schöne Schlacht
um seinen Eigensinn.
Er saß zu Pferde: ihm entging
keine Gebärde rings.
Auf Silber sprach jetzt Ring zu Ring,
und Stimme war in jedem Ding,
und wie in vielen Glocken hing
die Seele jedes Dings.
Und auch der Wind war anders groß,
der in die Fahnen sprang,
schlank wie ein Panther, atemlos
und taumelnd vom Trompetenstoß,
der lachend mit ihm rang.
Und manchmal griff der Wind hinab:
da ging ein Blutender, — ein Knab,
welcher die Trommel schlug;
er trug sie immer auf und ab
und trug sie wie sein Herz ins Grab
vor seinem toten Zug.
Da wurde mancher Berg geballt,
als wär die Erde noch nicht alt
und baute sich erst auf;
bald stand das Eisen wie Basalt,
bald schwankte wie ein Abendwald
mit breiter steigender Gestalt
der großbewegte Hauf.
Es dampfte dumpf die Dunkelheit,
was dunkelte war nicht die Zeit, —
und alles wurde grau,

and rode into a fierce resistance
and fought for love of danger
until the Miracle vanquished him:
as if dreaming his hand went
from coat of mail to coat of mail
and there was no sword in it;
he had been wakened into gazing:
the lovely battle stroked and flattered
at his willfulness.
He sat on horseback: no gesture
anywhere around escaped him.
Now link on link in silver talked,
and voice was in every object
and as if in many bell-chimes hung
the soul of each bright thing.
And the great wind was different too:
it *sprang* into the flags,
slim like a panther, breathless
and reeling from the trumpet-blast
that wrestled with it, laughing all the while.
And sometimes the wind swooped down:
there went one bleeding,—a boy
who beat the rallying-drum;
endlessly he bore it up and down
and bore it like his heart into the grave
before his company of dead.
There many a mountain was still clenched
as if the earth were not yet old
and were just now putting forth its forms;
now the iron stood fixed like basalt,
now the mightily moved pile
swayed like an evening forest
with vaster, ever-rising shape.
The darkness steamed, stifling,
what darkened was not time,—
and everything was turning gray,

aber schon fiel ein neues Scheit,
und wieder ward die Flamme breit
und festlich angefacht.
Sie griffen an: in fremder Tracht
ein Schwarm phantastischer Provinzen;
wie alles Eisen plötzlich lacht:
von einem silberlichten Prinzen
erschimmerte die Abendschlacht.
Die Fahnen flatterten wie Freuden,
und Alle hatten königlich
in ihren Gesten ein Vergeuden, —
an fernen flammenden Gebäuden
entzündeten die Sterne sich . . .

Und Nacht war. Und die Schlacht trat sachte
zurück wie ein sehr müdes Meer,
das viele fremde Tote brachte,
und alle Toten waren schwer.
Vorsichtig ging das graue Pferd
(von großen Fäusten abgewehrt)
durch Männer, welche fremd verstarben,
und trat auf flaches, schwarzes Gras.
Der auf dem grauen Pferde saß,
sah unten auf den feuchten Farben
viel Silber wie zerschelltes Glas.
Sah Eisen welken, Helme trinken
und Schwerter stehn in Panzernaht,
sterbende Hände sah er winken
mit einem Fetzen von Brokat . . .
Und sah es nicht.

Und ritt dem Lärme
der Feldschlacht nach, als ob er schwärme,
mit seinen Wangen voller Wärme
und mit den Augen von Verliebten . . .

but suddenly a new log fell,
and once again the flames fanned out
and raged for wild delights.
They all attacked: in strange attire
a swarm of unreal legions;
how all things iron laughed out:
the evening battle glittered
from some prince in silver mail.
The flags streamed like joys,
and everyone had in his gestures
a royal extravagance,—
from far-off burning buildings
the stars caught fire . . .

And night fell. And the battle ebbed softly
back like an exhausted sea
that carried many unknown dead ashore,
and all the dead were stone.
Cautiously the gray horse stepped
(by great fists fended off)
through men who died in foreign lands,
and it trod on flat, black grass.
He who sat on the gray horse
saw down below on the wet colors
endless silver like shattered glass.
Saw iron wilt, saw helmets drink,
saw swords rise out of armor-seams,
dying hands he saw waving
with some last remnant of brocade . . .
And saw it not.

And pursued on horse
the echoes of that din as if enraptured,
with his cheeks hot with passion
and with the eyes of lovers . . .

DER SOHN

Mein Vater war ein verbannter
König von überm Meer.
Ihm kam einmal ein Gesandter:
sein Mantel war ein Panther,
und sein Schwert war schwer.

Mein Vater war wie immer
ohne Helm und Hermelin;
es dunkelte das Zimmer
wie immer arm um ihn.

Es zitterten seine Hände
und waren blaß und leer, —
in bilderlose Wände
blicklos schaute er.

Die Mutter ging im Garten
und wandelte weiß im Grün,
und wollte den Wind erwarten
vor dem Abendglühn.
Ich träumte, sie würde mich rufen,
aber sie ging allein, —
ließ mich vom Rande der Stufen
horchen verhallenden Hufen
und ins Haus hinein:

Vater! Der fremde Gesandte . . . ?
Der reitet wieder im Wind . . .
Was wollte der? Er erkannte
dein blondes Haar, mein Kind.
Vater! Wie war er gekleidet!
Wie der Mantel von ihm floß!
Geschmiedet und geschmeidet

THE SON

My father was a banished king
from across the sea.
Once an envoy came here:
his cloak made him a panther,
and his sword was steel.

My father was, as he always was,
without crown and ermine;
around him the room lost luster
the way it always did.

His hands trembled
and were pale and empty,—
into walls without pictures
he blankly gazed.

My mother walked in the garden
and wandered all white through the green,
and felt for stirrings of that wind
before the evening glow.
I dreamed that she would call me,
but she walked alone,—
let me from the terrace's edge
hear fading hoofbeats
and turn back into the house:

Father! The foreign messenger . . . ?
Who rides again in the wind . . .
What did he want? He recognized
your blond hair, my child.
Father! The clothes he wore!
The way his cloak flowed from him!
Gem-studded and iron-sheathed

war Schulter, Brust und Roß.
Er war eine Stimme im Stahle,
er war ein Mann aus Nacht, —
aber er hat eine schmale
Krone mitgebracht.
Sie klang bei jedem Schritte
an sein sehr schweres Schwert,
die Perle in ihrer Mitte
ist viele Leben wert.
Vom zornigen Ergreifen
verbogen ist der Reifen,
der oft gefallen war:
es ist eine Kinderkrone, —
denn Könige sind ohne;
— gieb sie meinem Haar!
Ich will sie manchmal tragen
in Nächten, blaß vor Scham.
Und will dir, Vater, sagen,
woher der Gesandte kam.
Was dort die Dinge gelten,
ob steinern steht die Stadt,
oder ob man in Zelten
mich erwartet hat.

Mein Vater war ein Gekränkter
und kannte nur wenig Ruh.
Er hörte mir mit verhängter
Stirne nächtelang zu.
Mir lag im Haar der Ring.
Und ich sprach ganz nahe und sachte,
daß die Mutter nicht erwachte, —
die an dasselbe dachte,
wenn sie, ganz weiß gelassen,
vor abendlichen Massen
durch dunkle Gärten ging.

•

were shoulder, breast, and horse!
He was a voice inside steel,
he was a man made out of night,—
but what he brought here
was a narrow crown.
It rang with each step
against his massive sword,
the pearl in its center
must have cost many lives.
From being seized in fits of anger
that diadem is bent
which had so often fallen:
it is a child's crown,—
for kings are without one;
—let my hair have it!
I will put it on sometimes
at night, pale with shame.
And please, Father, tell me,
where the envoy came from.
What is it like there,
is the city walled in stone,
or in wind-blown tents
am I awaited?

My father was an aggrieved one
who knew little rest.
He listened to me with darkened
brow for nights on end.
The ring lay in my hair.
And I spoke up close and softly,
so as not to wake my mother,—
who thought about the same things
when she, left all in white,
before vague shapes of evening
walked through dark gardens.

•

... So wurden wir verträumte Geiger,
die leise aus den Türen treten,
um auszuschauen, eh sie beten,
ob nicht ein Nachbar sie belauscht.
Die erst, wenn alle sich zerstreuten,
hinter dem letzten Abendläuten,
die Lieder spielen, hinter denen
(wie Wald im Wind hinter Fontänen)
der dunkle Geigenkasten rauscht.
Denn dann nur sind die Stimmen gut,
wenn Schweigsamkeiten sie begleiten,
wenn hinter dem Gespräch der Saiten
Geräusche bleiben wie von Blut;
und bang und sinnlos sind die Zeiten,
wenn hinter ihren Eitelkeiten
nicht etwas waltet, welches ruht.

Geduld: es kreist der leise Zeiger,
und was verheißen ward, wird sein:
Wir sind die Flüstrer vor dem Schweiger,
wir sind die Wiesen vor dem Hain;
in ihnen geht noch dunkles Summen —
(viel Stimmen sind und doch kein Chor)
und sie bereiten auf die stummen
tiefen heiligen Haine vor ...

. . . Thus we became dreamy violinists,
who softly step out of doors
to make sure, before they pray,
that no neighbor eavesdrops on them.
Who only, when all have scattered,
behind the last evening sounds,
play the songs behind which
(like woods in the wind behind fountains)
the dark violin-case murmurs.
For the voices are only any good
when silences accompany them,
when behind the speech of the strings
sounds remain as if from blood;
and afraid and hollow are those times
when behind their vanities
no force presides that is at rest.

Patience: the gentle clock hand circles,
and what was promised once, will be:
We are the whisperers before the silent one,
we are the meadows before the wood;
in them a dark humming still runs—
(there are many voices and yet no choir)
and they prepare one for the mute, deep,
ever-present holy groves . . .

DIE ZAREN

Ein Gedicht-Kreis (1899 und 1906)

I

Das war in Tagen, da die Berge kamen:
die Bäume bäumten sich, die noch nicht zahmen,
und rauschend in die Rüstung stieg der Strom.
Zwei fremde Pilger riefen einen Namen,
und aufgewacht aus seinem langen Lahmen
war Ilija, der Riese von Murom.

Die alten Eltern brachen in den Äckern
an Steinen ab und an dem wilden Wuchs;
da kam der Sohn, ganz groß, von seinen Weckern
und zwang die Furchen in die Furcht des Pflugs.
Er hob die Stämme, die wie Streiter standen,
und lachte ihres wankenden Gewichts,
und aufgestört wie schwarze Schlangen wanden
die Wurzeln, welche nur das Dunkel kannten,
sich in dem breiten Griff des Lichts.

Es stärkte sich im frühen Tau die Mähre,
in deren Adern Kraft und Adel schlief;
sie reifte unter ihres Reiters Schwere,
ihr Wiehern war wie eine Stimme tief, —
und beide fühlten, wie das Ungefähre
sie mit verheißenden Gefahren rief.

Und reiten, reiten . . . vielleicht tausend Jahre.
Wer zählt die Zeit, wenn einmal Einer will.
(Vielleicht saß er auch tausend Jahre still.)
Das Wirkliche ist wie das Wunderbare:

THE TSARS
A Poem Cycle (1899 and 1906)

I

That was in days when the mountains came:
the trees, which were not yet docile, reared up,
and roaring into ramparts the river rose.
Two foreign pilgrims shouted a name,
and out of his long crippledness
arose Ilya, the giant of Muron.

The old parents labored in the fields
breaking stones and hacking out wild growth;
then the son came, immense, from being wakened,
and forced the furrows to obey the plow.
He lifted the tree trunks, which stood like fighters,
and laughed at their tottering weight,
while their roots, stirred up like black snakes,
having only known the darkness
writhed and twisted in the light's broad grip.

The early dew brought vigor to the mare,
in whose veins strength and nobility slept;
she matured under her rider's heaviness,
her neighing was full and deep, like a voice,—
and both felt how things dimly glimpsed
called them with auspicious dangers.

And rode, rode . . . perhaps a thousand years.
Who counts the time, when someone simply wills.
(Perhaps he also sat still a thousand years.)
The real is like the miraculous:

es mißt die Welt mit eigenmächtigen Maßen;
Jahrtausende sind ihm zu jung.

Weit schreiten werden, welche lange saßen
in ihrer tiefen Dämmerung.

it takes the world exactly as it pleases:
millennia are too young for it.

Far shall they stride who for long hours sat
in their being's deep twilight.

Noch drohen große Vögel allenthalben,
und Drachen glühn und hüten überall
der Wälder Wunder und der Schluchten Fall;
und Knaben wachsen an, und Männer salben
sich zu dem Kampfe mit der Nachtigall,

die oben in den Kronen von neun Eichen
sich lagert wie ein tausendfaches Tier,
und abends geht ein Schreien ohnegleichen,
ein schreiendes Bis-an-das-Ende-Reichen,
und geht die ganze Nacht lang aus von ihr;

die Frühlingsnacht, die schrecklicher als alles
und schwerer war und banger zu bestehn:
ringsum kein Zeichen eines Überfalles
und dennoch alles voller Übergehn,
hinwerfend sich und Stück für Stück sich gebend,
ja jenes Etwas, welches um sich griff,
anrufend noch, am ganzen Leibe bebend
und darin untergehend wie ein Schiff.

Das waren Überstarke, die da blieben,
von diesem Riesigen nicht aufgerieben,
das aus den Kehlen wie aus Kratern brach;
sie dauerten, und alternd nach und nach
begriffen sie die Bangnis der Aprile,
und ihre ruhigen Hände hielten viele
und führten sie durch Furcht und Ungemach
zu Tagen, da sie froher und gesünder
die Mauern bauten um die Städtegründer,
die über allem gut und kundig saßen.

II

Great birds still threaten on all sides,
and dragons glow and guard with darkest care
the forest's marvel and the gorge's fall;
and boys grow up, and men anoint themselves
to fight the battle with the nightingale,

who high up in the crowns of nine oaks
camps like a thousand-sided animal,
and at evening a shriek issues out of it
that pierces to the very end, a weird
unearthly shriek that goes on all night long:

that spring night, most terrible of all
and hardest and most frightening to outlast:
all around no signs of any ambush,
and yet everything rife with transformation,
casting itself down and piecemeal giving itself over,
even that Something which was breaking up,
still calling, its entire body trembling
and going under in it like a ship.

Those were supremely strong ones, who *stayed* there,
not worn down by that immensity
that out of throats as out of craters broke;
they *lasted*, and aging bit by bit
they grasped the dread that Aprils held,
and their peaceable hands took many
and led them through fear and hardship
to days when they, more resilient,
built their walls around the city founders,
who sat wisely and ably over everyone.

Und schließlich kamen auf den ersten Straßen
aus Höhlen und verhaßten Hinterhalten
die Tiere, die für unerbittlich galten.
Sie stiegen still aus ihren Übermaßen
(beschämte und veraltete Gewalten)
und legten sich gehorsam vor die Alten.

And finally, down the first streets,
out of lairs and detested lurking-places,
came the animals deemed intractable.
They climbed quietly out of their excesses
(shamed and antiquated violences)
and lay obediently at the elders' feet.

Seine Diener füttern mit mehr und mehr
ein Rudel von jenen wilden Gerüchten,
die auch noch Er sind, alles noch Er.

Seine Günstlinge flüchten vor ihm her.

Und seine Frauen flüstern und stiften
Bünde. Und er hört sie ganz innen
in ihren Gemächern mit Dienerinnen,
die sich scheu umsehn, sprechen von Giften.

Alle Wände sind hohl von Schränken und Fächern,
Mörder ducken unter den Dächern
und spielen Mönche mit viel Geschick.

Und er hat nichts als einen Blick
dann und wann; als den leisen
Schritt auf den Treppen die kreisen;
nichts als das Eisen an seinem Stock.

Nichts als den dürftigen Büßerrock
(durch den die Kälte aus den Fliesen
an ihm hinaufkriecht wie mit Krallen)
nichts, was er zu rufen wagt,
nichts als die Angst vor allen diesen,
nichts als die tägliche Angst vor Allen,
die ihn jagt durch diese gejagten
Gesichter, an dunklen ungefragten
vielleicht schuldigen Händen entlang.

Manchmal packt er Einen im Gang
grade noch an des Mantels Falten,

III

His servants feed with more and more
a flock of those wild rumors
that are still Him, everything still Him.

His favorites flee before him.

And his wives whisper and create
alliances. And he hears them far inside
in their chambers with waiting-women,
who glance furtively, speak of poison.

All walls are hollow behind shelves and panels,
murderers crouch beneath the roofs
and play the monk most skillfully.

And he has nothing more than a glimpse
now and then; nothing more than the soft
step on the stairs that spiral upward;
nothing more than the iron on his stick.

Nothing more than the thin penitential gown
(through which the cold from the tiles
creeps up around him as with claws),
nothing that he dares to call,
nothing but the fear of all of these,
nothing but the daily fear of everything,
which hounds him through these hounded
faces, hounds him on past dark unquestioned
perhaps already guilty hands.

Sometimes he seizes someone in the corridor
just in time by his mantle's folds

und er zerrt ihn zornig her;
aber im Fenster weiß er nicht mehr:
wer ist Haltender? Wer ist gehalten?
Wer bin ich und wer ist der?

and drags him furiously in;
but at the window he no longer knows:
Who is the holder? Who is held?
Who am I and who is he?

IV

Es ist die Stunde, da das Reich sich eitel
in seines Glanzes vielen Spiegeln sieht.

Der blasse Zar, des Stammes letztes Glied,
träumt auf dem Thron, davor das Fest geschieht,
und leise zittert sein beschämter Scheitel
und seine Hand, die vor den Purpurlehnen
mit einem unbestimmten Sehnen
ins wirre Ungewisse flieht.

Und um sein Schweigen neigen sich Bojaren
in blanken Panzern und in Pantherfellen,
wie viele fremde fürstliche Gefahren,
die ihn mit stummer Ungeduld umstellen.
Tief in den Saal schlägt ihre Ehrfurcht Wellen.

Und sie gedenken eines andern Zaren,
der oft mit Worten, die aus Wahnsinn waren,
ihnen die Stirnen an die Steine stieß.
Und denken also weiter: *jener* ließ
nicht so viel Raum, wenn er zu Throne saß,
auf dem verwelkten Samt des Kissens leer.

Er war der Dinge dunkles Maß,
und die Bojaren wußten lang nicht mehr,
daß rot der Sitz des Sessels sei, so schwer
lag sein Gewand und wurde golden breit.

Und weiter denken sie: das Kaiserkleid
schläft auf den Schultern dieses Knaben ein.
Obgleich im ganzen Saal die Fackeln flacken,
sind bleich die Perlen, die in sieben Reihn,

IV

It is the hour when the empire vainly
gazes into its splendor's many mirrors.

The pale Tsar, his clan's last member,
dreams on the throne before the pageantry,
and his shamed locks faintly tremble
and his hand also, which flees before the purpled
armrests with a chaotic longing
into pathless uncertainty.

And around his silence boyars bow
in shining armor and in panther skins,
like many strange royal dangers
that surround him with mute impatience.
Deep into the hall their awe breaks like waves.

And they call to mind a different Tsar,
who often with words made out of madness
thrust their brows against the stones.
And then think further: that one didn't leave,
when he ruled from the throne, so much space empty
on the faded velvet of the pillows.

He was the entire world's dark measure,
and the boyars had long ceased to be aware
that the chair's seat was red, the way
his cloak in all its goldenness spread wide.

And they keep on thinking: the Kaiser's garb
sleeps on the shoulders of this boy.
Although the torches flare throughout the hall,
the pearls are pale that in seven rows,

wie weiße Kinder, knien um seinen Nacken,
und die Rubine an den Ärmelzacken,
die einst Pokale waren, klar von Wein,
sind schwarz wie Schlacken —

Und ihr Denken schwillt.

Es drängt sich heftig an den blassen Kaiser,
auf dessen Haupt die Krone immer leiser
und dem der Wille immer fremder wird;
er lächelt. Lauter prüfen ihn die Preiser,
ihr Neigen nähert sich, sie schmeicheln heiser,
und eine Klinge hat im Traum geklirrt.

like white children, kneel around his neck,
and the rubies on the sleeve-serrations,
once goblets bright with wine,
are black as cinders—

And their thinking swells.

It crowds in against the pale Emperor,
on whose head the crown grows ever lighter
and from whom the will grows ever more estranged;
he smiles. The praisers test him more loudly,
their bowing draws closer, they flatter more hoarsely—
and a blade has been unsheathed in dream.

V

Der blasse Zar wird nicht am Schwerte sterben,
die fremde Sehnsucht macht ihn sakrosankt;
er wird die feierlichen Reiche erben,
an denen seine sanfte Seele krankt.

Schon jetzt, hintretend an ein Kremlfenster,
sieht er ein Moskau, weißer, unbegrenzter,
in seine endlich fertige Nacht gewebt;
so wie es ist im ersten Frühlingswirken,
wenn in den Gassen der Geruch aus Birken
von lauter Morgenglocken bebt.

Die großen Glocken, die so herrisch lauten,
sind seine Väter, jene ersten Zaren,
die sie noch vor den Tagen der Tartaren
aus Sagen, Abenteuern und Gefahren,
aus Zorn und Demut zögernd auferbauten.

Und er begreift auf einmal, wer sie waren,
und daß sie oft um ihres Dunkels Sinn
in *seine* eignen Tiefen niedertauchten
und ihn, den Leisesten von den Erlauchten,
in ihren Taten groß und fromm verbrauchten
schon lang vor seinem Anbeginn.

Und eine Dankbarkeit kommt über ihn,
daß sie ihn so verschwenderisch vergeben
an aller Dinge Durst und Drang.
Er war die Kraft zu ihrem Überschwang,
der goldne Grund, vor dem ihr breites Leben
geheimnisvoll zu dunkeln schien.

V

The pale Tsar will not die by the sword,
the strange longing makes him sacrosanct;
he will inherit the festive kingdoms
with which his gentle soul is so afflicted.

Already now, stepping toward a Kremlin window,
he sees a Moscow, whiter, less separate,
worked into its finally finished night;
the way it is in the first spring weavings,
when through the streets the scent from birch trees
trembles with endless morning bells.

The great bells, which ring imperiously,
are his fathers, those first tsars,
who even in the days before the Tartars
from legends, perils, and adventures,
from rage and humility hesitantly arose.

And he grasps suddenly who they were,
and that they often, to give their darkness sense,
dived down into *his* own depths
and used him, the gentlest of the anointed,
greatly and devoutly in their deeds
long before his own life came.

And suddenly he feels a great thankfulness
that they so lavishly bestowed him
on all things' thirst and urge.
He was the strength for their exuberance,
the golden ground against which their broad lives
mysteriously appeared to darken.

In allen ihren Werken schaut er *sich*,
wie eingelegtes Silber in Zieraten,
und es giebt keine Tat in ihren Taten,
die nicht auch *war* in seinen stillen Staaten,
in denen alles Handelns Rot verblich.

In all their works he sees *himself,*
like inlaid silver in the finest handcraft,
and there is no deed in their doings
that wasn't also there in his still states,
in which all action's red turned pale.

VI

Noch immer schauen in den Silberplatten
wie tiefe Frauenaugen die Saphire,
Goldranken schlingen sich wie schlanke Tiere,
die sich im Glanze ihrer Brünste gatten,
und sanfte Perlen warten in dem Schatten
wilder Gebilde, daß ein Schimmer ihre
stillen Gesichter finde und verliere.
Und das ist Mantel, Strahlenkranz und Land,
und ein Bewegen geht von Rand zu Rand,
wie Korn im Wind und wie ein Fluß im Tale,
so glänzt es wechselnd durch die Rahmenwand.

In ihrer Sonne dunkeln drei Ovale:
das große giebt dem Mutterantlitz Raum,
und rechts und links hebt eine mandelschmale
Jungfrauenhand sich aus dem Silbersaum.
Die beiden Hände, seltsam still und braun,
verkünden, daß im köstlichen Ikone
die Königliche wie im Kloster wohne,
die überfließen wird von jenem Sohne,
von jenem Tropfen, drinnen wolkenohne
die niegehofften Himmel blaun.

Die Hände zeugen noch dafür;
aber das Antlitz ist wie eine Tür
in warme Dämmerungen aufgegangen,
in die das Lächeln von den Gnadenwangen
mit seinem Lichte irrend, sich verlor.
Da neigt sich tief der Zar davor und spricht:

Fühltest Du nicht, wie sehr wir in Dich drangen
mit allem Fühlen, Fürchten und Verlangen:

Still in the surrounding silver-plating
sapphires gaze like deep female eyes,
gold tendrils coil together like slim panthers
that mate in the brilliance of their heat,
and soft pearls wait in the shadows
of wild designs, so that a glimmer might
briefly light their silent faces.
And all this is mantle, aureole, and land,
and movement runs from edge to edge,—
like corn in wind, like rivers in a valley,
light ripples through the jeweled sheath.

Within their sun three ovals darken:
the large one leaves the mother's face a space,
and left and right an almond-slender
virgin hand rises out of the silver sleeve.
The two hands, oddly quiet and brown,
announce that in the priceless icon
dwells, as in a cloister, the royal lady
who will be overflowing with that son,
with that drop, within which, free of clouds,
the never-hoped-for skies turn blue.

The hands still witness to it;
but the countenance is like a door
opened out into warm twilight,
in which the smile of the forgiving cheeks,
straying with its light, got lost.
The Tsar kneels deep before it, speaks:

    Did You not feel how we thronged into You
    with all feelings, longings, and forebodings:

wir warten auf Dein liebes Angesicht,
das uns vergangen ist; wohin vergangen?:

Den großen Heiligen vergeht es nicht.

Er bebte tief in seinem steifen Kleid,
das strahlend stand. Er wußte nicht, wie weit
er schon von allem war, und ihrem Segnen
wie selig nah in seiner Einsamkeit.

Noch sinnt und sinnt der blasse Gossudar.
Und sein Gesicht, das unterm kranken Haar
schon lange tief und wie im Fortgehn war,
verging, wie jenes in dem Goldovale,
in seinem großen goldenen Talar.

(Um ihrem Angesichte zu begegnen.)

Zwei Goldgewänder schimmerten im Saale
und wurden in dem Glanz der Ampeln klar.

we wait for Your loving countenance
that has vanished from us; vanished where?:

For the great saints it doesn't vanish.

He trembled deeply in his stiff robe
that stood shining. He didn't know how far
he was by now from everything, and how close
in his solitude to her benediction.

Still the pale Gossudar broods and broods.
And his face, which under sickly hair
and in his great golden talar has already
long been deep and as if engaged in leaving,
passed on, like the one in the gold oval.

(In order to meet her countenance.)

Two golden garments shimmered in the hall
and in the gleam of hanging lamps grew bright.

DER SÄNGER SINGT VOR
EINEM FÜRSTENKIND
Dem Andenken von Paula Becker-Modersohn

Du blasses Kind, an jedem Abend soll
der Sänger dunkel stehn bei deinen Dingen
und soll dir Sagen, die im Blute klingen,
über die Brücke seiner Stimme bringen
und eine Harfe, seiner Hände voll.

Nicht aus der Zeit ist, was er dir erzählt,
gehoben ist es wie aus Wandgeweben;
solche Gestalten hat es nie gegeben, —
und Niegewesenes nennt er das Leben.
Und heute hat er diesen Sang erwählt:

Du blondes Kind von Fürsten und aus Frauen,
die einsam warteten im weißen Saal, —
fast alle waren bang, dich aufzubauen,
um aus den Bildern einst auf dich zu schauen:
auf deine Augen mit den ernsten Brauen,
auf deine Hände, hell und schmal.

Du hast von ihnen Perlen und Türkisen,
von diesen Frauen, die in Bildern stehn
als stünden sie allein in Abendwiesen, —
du hast von ihnen Perlen und Türkisen
und Ringe mit verdunkelten Devisen
und Seiden, welche welke Düfte wehn.

Du trägst die Gemmen ihrer Gürtelbänder
ans hohe Fenster in den Glanz der Stunden,
und in die Seide sanfter Brautgewänder
sind deine kleinen Bücher eingebunden,
und drinnen hast du, mächtig über Länder,

THE SINGER SINGS BEFORE
A CHILD OF PRINCES
In Memory of Paula Becker-Modersohn

You pale child, each evening the singer
shall stand darkly among your things
and bring you, over his voice's bridge,
legends that ring out in the blood,
and a harp filled with his artful hands.

Not out of time comes what he tells you,
it is lifted as out of tapestries;
such figures have never had existence,—
and he calls what never existed life.
And today he has picked for you this song:

You blond child of princes and out of women
who waited solitary in the white hall,—
all, almost, were afraid to aid your making,
in order one day to gaze on you out of portraits:
on your eyes, with their serious brows,
on your hands, bright and thin.

You have from them pearls and richest turquoise,
from these women who stand in portraits
as though they stood alone in evening meadows,—
you have from them pearls and richest turquoise
and rings with enigmatic mottoes
and silks, which waft faded fragrance.

You bear the gems from their waistbands
past the high window into the hours' brilliance,
and in the silk of soft bridal garments
your small books are bound,
and there inside, written very large and with rich,

ganz groß geschrieben und mit reichen, runden
Buchstaben deinen Namen vorgefunden.

Und alles ist, als wär es schon geschehn.

Sie haben so, als ob du nicht mehr kämst,
an alle Becher ihren Mund gesetzt,
zu allen Freuden ihr Gefühl gehetzt
und keinem Leide leidlos zugesehn;
so daß du jetzt
stehst und dich schämst.

. . . Du blasses Kind, dein Leben ist auch eines, —
der Sänger kommt dir sagen, daß du bist.
Und daß du mehr bist als ein Traum des Haines,
mehr als die Seligkeit des Sonnenscheines,
den mancher graue Tag vergißt.
Dein Leben ist so unaussprechlich Deines,
weil es von vielen überladen ist.

Empfindest du, wie die Vergangenheiten
leicht werden, wenn du eine Weile lebst,
wie sie dich sanft auf Wunder vorbereiten,
jedes Gefühl mit Bildern dir begleiten, —
und nur ein Zeichen scheinen ganze Zeiten
für eine Geste, die du schön erhebst. —

Das ist der Sinn von allem, was einst war,
daß es nich bleibt mit seiner ganzen Schwere,
daß es zu unserm Wesen wiederkehre,
in uns verwoben, tief und wunderbar:

So waren diese Frauen elfenbeinern,
von vielen Rosen rötlich angeschienen,
so dunkelten die müden Königsmienen,
so wurden fahle Fürstenmunde steinern

round letters, you, mighty over lands,
have come upon your name.

And it's as if the past claimed everything.

They have—as if your coming were annulled—
on every goblet placed their lips,
toward every pleasure whipped their feeling,
and on no grief gazed painlessly;
so that you now stand here
and feel ashamed.

. . . You pale child, yours also is a life,—
the singer comes to tell you that you *are*.
And that you are more than a dream of the forest,
more than the blessedness of sunshine
which many a gray day forgets.
Your life is so inexpressibly your own
because it is laden with so many.

Can you not sometimes feel how all pasts
grow light, when you've lived a while,
how they gently prepare you for amazement,
companion each feeling with images,—
and how whole eras seem but a sign
for some lovely gesture that you raise.—

This is the crux of all that once existed:
that it does not remain with all its weight,
that to our being it returns instead,
woven into us, deep and magical:

Thus were these women as of ivory,
by many roses redly shone upon,
thus darkened the weary mien of kings,
thus sallow mouths of princes turned to stone

und unbewegt von Waisen und von Weinern,
so klangen Knaben an wie Violinen
und starben für der Frauen schweres Haar;
so gingen Jungfraun der Madonna dienen,
denen die Welt verworren war.
So wurden Lauten laut und Mandolinen,
in die ein Unbekannter größer griff, —
in warmen Samt verlief der Dolche Schliff, —
Schicksale bauten sich aus Glück und Glauben,
Abschiede schluchzten auf in Abendlauben, —
und über hundert schwarzen Eisenhauben
schwankte die Feldschlacht wie ein Schiff.
So wurden Städte langsam groß und fielen
in sich zurück wie Wellen eines Meeres,
so drängte sich zu hochbelohnten Zielen
die rasche Vogelkraft des Eisenspeeres,
so schmückten Kinder sich zu Gartenspielen, —
und so geschah Unwichtiges und Schweres,
nur, um für dieses tägliche Erleben
dir tausend große Gleichnisse zu geben,
an denen du gewaltig wachsen kannst.

Vergangenheiten sind dir eingepflanzt,
um sich aus dir, wie Gärten, zu erheben.

Du blasses Kind, du machst den Sänger reich
mit deinem Schicksal, das sich singen läßt:
so spiegelt sich ein großes Gartenfest
mit vielen Lichtern im erstaunten Teich.
Im dunklen Dichter wiederholt sich still
ein jedes Ding: ein Stern, ein Haus, ein Wald.
Und viele Dinge, die er feiern will,
umstehen deine rührende Gestalt.

and were unmoved by orphans and by weepers,
thus boys longed like violins
and died for the heavy hair of women;
thus virgins for whom the world was wild
dedicated themselves to the Madonna.
Thus lutes and mandolins grew loud
in some unknown player's greater span,—
into warm velvet slipped the polished blade,—
destinies built up from faith and fortune,
farewells sobbed in evening arbors,—
and over hundreds of black iron helmets
the battle on the plain pitched like a ship.
Thus cities grew slowly great and fell
back into themselves like ocean waves,
thus the swift bird-strength of the iron spear
hurled itself toward high-rewarded goals,
thus children dressed themselves for garden games,—
and thus things trivial and hard took place,
only to give you for this daily living
a thousand great similes and likenesses,
by which you prodigiously may grow.

Past upon past has been planted in you,
in order out of you, like a garden, to rise.

You pale child, you enrich the singer
with your fate, whose praises may be sung:
thus a huge garden-party is mirrored
with many lights in the astonished pond.
In the dark poet each thing silently
repeats itself: a star, a house, a forest.
And many things that he would celebrate
stand all around your moving form.

DIE AUS DEM HAUSE COLONNA

Ihr fremden Männer, die ihr jetzt so still
in Bildern steht, ihr saßen gut zu Pferde
und ungeduldig gingt ihr durch das Haus;
wie ein schöner Hund, mit derselben Gebärde
ruhn eure Hände jetzt bei euch aus.

Euer Gesicht is so voll von Schauen,
denn die Welt war euch Bild und Bild;
aus Waffen, Fahnen, Früchten und Frauen
quillt euch dieses große Vertrauen,
daß alles *ist* und daß alles *gilt*.

Aber damals, als ihr noch zu jung
wart, die großen Schlachten zu schlagen,
zu jung, um den päpstlichen Purpur zu tragen,
nicht immer glücklich bei Reiten und Jagen,
Knaben noch, die sich den Frauen versagen,
habt ihr aus jenen Knabentagen
keine, nicht eine Erinnerung?

Wißt ihr nicht mehr, was damals war?

Damals war der Altar
mit dem Bilde, auf dem Maria gebar,
in dem einsamen Seitenschiff.
Euch ergriff
eine Blumenranke;
der Gedanke,
daß die Fontäne allein
draußen im Garten in Mondenschein
ihre Wasser warf,
war wie eine Welt.

THOSE OF THE HOUSE OF COLONNA

You far-off men, who stand now so motionless
in portraits, you sat at ease on horseback
and impatiently you strode through the hall;
like a great dog, with that same gesture
your hands now rest beside you.

Your face is so filled with gazing,
because for you the world was picture and picture;
out of armor, flags, ripe fruit, and women
welled for you that great confidence
that everything *is* and *counts*.

But back then when you were still too young
to lead your forces in the great battles,
too young to wear the robes of papal crimson,
not always favored in riding and hunting,
boys still, who forswore the charms of women,
have you from all those boyhood days
not one, not a single memory?

Have you forgotten how life felt back then?

Back then the altar, with its painting
on which Mary gave birth, was tucked away
in the solitary side aisle.
You were enthralled
by a flower tendril;
the thought
that the fountain all alone
outside in the garden bathed in moonlight
cast its water skyward
was like a world.

Das Fenster ging bis zu den Füßen auf wie eine Tür;
und es war Park mit Wiesen und Wegen:
seltsam nah und doch so entlegen,
seltsam hell und doch wie verborgen,
und die Brunnen rauschten wie Regen,
und es war, als käme kein Morgen
dieser langen Nacht entgegen,
die mit allen Sternen stand.

Damals wuchs euch, Knaben, die Hand,
die warm war. (Ihr aber wußtet es nicht.)
Damals breitete euer Gesicht sich aus.

The window opened right up to your feet like a door;
and all was park with lawns and paths:
strangely near and yet so far away,
strangely bright and yet as if concealed,
and the springs had voices like rain,
and it was as if no morning came
to meet that long night
which stood with all its stars.

Back then, boys, your hands *grew*,
and were warm. (But you didn't know it.)
Back then your faces burgeoned wide.

The Second Book, PART TWO

FRAGMENTE AUS VERLORENEN TAGEN

... Wie Vögel, welche sich gewöhnt ans Gehn
und immer schwerer werden, wie im Fallen:
die Erde saugt aus ihren langen Krallen
die mutige Erinnerung von allen
den großen Dingen, welche hoch geschehn,
und macht sie fast zu Blättern, die sich dicht
am Boden halten, —
wie Gewächse, die,
kaum aufwärts wachsend, in die Erde kriechen,
in schwarzen Schollen unlebendig licht
und weich und feucht versinken und versiechen, —
wie irre Kinder, — wie ein Angesicht
in einem Sarg, — wie frohe Hände, welche
unschlüssig werden, weil im vollen Kelche
sich Dinge spiegeln, die nicht nahe sind, —
wie Hülferufe, die im Abendwind
begegnen vielen dunklen großen Glocken, —
wie Zimmerblumen, die seit Tagen trocken,
wie Gassen, die verrufen sind, — wie Locken,
darinnen Edelsteine blind geworden sind, —
wie Morgen im April
vor allen vielen Fenstern des Spitales:
die Kranken drängen sich am Saum des Saales
und schaun: die Gnade eines frühen Strahles
macht alle Gassen frühlinglich und weit;
sie sehen nur die helle Herrlichkeit,
welche die Häuser jung und lachend macht,
und wissen nicht, daß schon die ganze Nacht
ein Sturm die Kleider von den Himmeln reißt,
ein Sturm von Wassern, wo die Welt noch eist,
ein Sturm, der jetzt noch durch die Gassen braust
und der den Dingen alle Bürde
von ihren Schultern nimmt, —

FRAGMENTS FROM LOST DAYS

. . . Like birds that get used to walking
and grow heavier and heavier, as in falling:
the earth sucks out of their long claws
the brave memory of all
the great things that happen high up,
and makes them almost into leaves that cling
tightly to the ground,—
like plants which,
scarcely growing upward, creep into the earth,
sink lightly and softly and damply
into black clods and sicken there lifelessly,—
like mad children,—like a face
in a coffin,—like happy hands that
grow hesitant, because in the full goblet
things are mirrored that are not near,—
like calls for help which in the evening wind
collide with many dark huge chimes,—
like house plants that have dried for days,
like streets that are ill-famed,—like bright curls
within which jewels have grown blind,—
like early morning in April
facing the hospital's many windows:
the sick press up against the hall's seam
and look: the grace of a new light
makes all the streets seem vernal and wide;
they see only the bright majesty
that makes the houses young and laughing,
and don't know that all night long
a storm ripped the garments from the sky,
a storm of waters, where the world still freezes,
a storm which this very moment roars through the streets
and takes all burdens
off the shoulders of each thing,—

daß Etwas draußen groß ist und ergrimmt,
daß draußen die Gewalt geht, eine Faust,
die jeden von den Kranken würgen würde
inmitten dieses Glanzes, dem sie glauben. —
... Wie lange Nächte in verwelkten Lauben,
die schon zerrissen sind auf allen Seiten
und viel zu weit, um noch mit einem Zweiten,
den man sehr liebt, zusammen drin zu weinen, —
wie nackte Mädchen, kommend über Steine,
wie Trunkene in einem Birkenhaine, —
wie Worte, welche nichts Bestimmtes meinen
und dennoch gehn, ins Ohr hineingehn, weiter
ins Hirn und heimlich auf der Nervenleiter
durch alle Glieder Sprung um Sprung versuchen, —
wie Greise, welche ihr Geschlecht verfluchen
und dann versterben, so daß keiner je
abwenden könnte das verhängte Weh,
wie volle Rosen, künstlich aufgezogen
im blauen Treibhaus, wo die Lüfte logen,
und dann vom Übermut in großem Bogen
hinausgestreut in den verwehten Schnee, —
wie eine Erde, die nicht kreisen kann,
weil zuviel Tote ihr Gefühl beschweren,
wie ein erschlagener verscharrter Mann,
dem sich die Hände gegen Wurzeln wehren, —
wie eine von den hohen, schlanken, roten
Hochsommerblumen, welche unerlöst
ganz plötzlich stirbt im Lieblingswind der Wiesen,
weil ihre Wurzel unten an Türkisen
im Ohrgehänge einer Toten
stößt ...

Und mancher Tage Stunden waren *so*.
Als formte wer mein Abbild irgendwo,

that Something outside is huge and incensed,
that outside Power stalks, a fist
that would strangle each one of the sick
in the midst of this brilliance, which they believe.—
. . . Like long nights in withered garden-huts,
which are already torn apart on all sides
and much too open now to weep there together
with another person, who is so loved,—
like naked girls, tiptoeing over stones,
like drunkards in a birch grove,—
like words which mean nothing definite
and yet go, go inside the ear, keep going
into the brain and secretly on the nerve-branches
through every limb try out leap after leap,—
like old men who curse their race
and then die, so that no one can ever
turn aside the once-pronounced woe,
like full roses, artfully raised
in the blue hothouse where the air lied,
and then from the exhilaration in great curves
strewn out upon the scattered snow,—
like an earth which cannot orbit,
because too many dead weigh on its feeling,
like a man killed and buried
whose hands defend themselves against roots,—
like one of the high, slim, red
midsummer flowers, which unredeemed
all at once dies in its favorite meadow-wind,
because down below its roots hit turquoise
in the earring of a corpse
and stop . . .

And many a day's hours were like that.
As if someone fashioned my likeness somewhere

um es mit Nadeln langsam zu mißhandeln.
Ich spürte jede Spitze seiner Spiele,
und war, als ob ein Regen auf mich fiele,
in welchem alle Dinge sich verwandeln.

in order to torment it slowly with needles.
I felt each sharp prick of his playing,
and it was: as if a rain fell on me
in which all things change.

DIE STIMMEN
Neun Blätter mit einem Titelblatt

TITELBLATT

Die Reichen und Glücklichen haben gut schweigen,
niemand will wissen was sie sind.
Aber die Dürftigen müssen sich zeigen,
müssen sagen: ich bin blind
oder: ich bin im Begriff es zu werden
oder: es geht mir nicht gut auf Erden
oder: ich habe ein krankes Kind
oder: da bin ich zusammengefügt . . .

Und vielleicht, daß das gar nicht genügt.

Und weil alle sonst, wie an Dingen,
an ihnen vorbeigehn, müssen sie singen.

Und da hört man noch guten Gesang.

Freilich die Menschen sind seltsam; sie hören
lieber Kastraten in Knabenchören.

Aber Gott selber kommt und bleibt lang
wenn ihn *diese* Beschnittenen stören.

THE VOICES

Nine Leaves with a Title Leaf

TITLE LEAF

The rich and the fortunate can well keep quiet,
nobody wants to know what they are.
But the destitute have to show themselves,
have to say: I am blind
or: I am about to become so
or: nothing on earth works out for me
or: I have a sick child
or: right here I am pieced together . . .

And perhaps even that won't suffice.

And since otherwise people pass by them
the way they pass things, they have to sing.

And the songs you hear there can be really good.

True, human beings are strange; they'd rather
hear castrati in boys' choirs.

But God himself comes and stays a long time
whenever *these* maimed ones bother him.

DAS LIED DES BETTLERS

Ich gehe immer von Tor zu Tor,
verregnet und verbrannt;
auf einmal leg ich mein rechtes Ohr
in meine rechte Hand.
Dann kommt mir meine Stimme vor
als hätt ich sie nie gekannt.

Dann weiß ich nicht sicher wer da schreit,
ich oder irgendwer.
Ich schreie um eine Kleinigkeit.
Die Dichter schrein um mehr.

Und endlich mach ich noch mein Gesicht
mit beiden Augen zu;
wie's dann in der Hand liegt mit seinem Gewicht
sieht es fast aus wie Ruh.
Damit sie nicht meinen ich hätte nicht,
wohin ich mein Haupt tu.

THE SONG OF THE BEGGAR

I go always from door to door,
rain-drenched and sun-scorched;
suddenly I'll lay my right ear
in my right hand.
Then my voice sounds to me
as if I'd never heard it.

Then I don't know for sure who screams there,
me or someone else.
I scream for some small trifle.
The poets scream for more.

And finally I'll close my face up
with both my eyes;
the way it lies then in my hand with its weight
it looks almost like rest.
So they won't think I hadn't any place
to put my head.

Ich bin blind, ihr draußen, das ist ein Fluch,
ein Widerwillen, ein Widerspruch,
etwas täglich Schweres.
Ich leg meine Hand auf den Arm der Frau,
meine graue Hand auf ihr graues Grau,
und sie führt mich durch lauter Leeres.

Ihr rührt euch und rückt und bildet euch ein
anders zu klingen als Stein auf Stein,
aber ihr irrt euch: ich allein
lebe und leide und lärme.
In mir ist ein endloses Schrein
und ich weiß nicht, schreit mir mein
Herz oder meine Gedärme.

Erkennt ihr die Lieder? Ihr sanget sie nicht,
nicht ganz in dieser Betonung.
Euch kommt jeden Morgen das neue Licht
warm in die offene Wohnung.
Und ihr habt ein Gefühl von Gesicht zu Gesicht
und das verleitet zur Schonung.

THE SONG OF THE BLIND MAN

I am blind, you out there, that is a curse,
a countermanding, a contradiction,
something daily weighing down.
I place my hand on the woman's arm,
my gray hand on her gray grayness,
and she leads me through nothing but void.

You move and shift and like to think
that you ring differently from stone on stone,
but you're wrong: I alone
live and suffer and make noise.
Inside me there's an endless screaming,
and I don't know if it's my heart
or my gut that screams.

Recognize the songs? You never sang them,
not with this accent anyway.
For you every morning the new light comes
warmly into your open lodging.
And you have a feeling of face to face,
and that entices you to caring.

DAS LIED DES TRINKERS

Es war nicht in mir. Es ging aus und ein.
Da wollt ich es halten. Da hielt es der Wein.
(Ich weiß nicht mehr was es war.)
Dann hielt er mir jenes und hielt mir dies
bis ich mich ganz auf ihn verließ.
Ich Narr.

Jetzt bin ich in seinem Spiel und er streut
mich verächtlich herum und verliert mich noch heut
an dieses Vieh, an den Tod.
Wenn der mich, schmutzige Karte, gewinnt,
so kratzt er mit mir seinen grauen Grind
und wirft mich fort in den Kot.

It was not in me. It went out and in.
Then I tried to hold it. Then the wine held it.
(I don't know any more what it was.)
Then the wine held me this and held me that,
till I totally relied on it.
I, fool.

Now I am in its game and it strews
me scornfully about and loses me this day
to that loutish swine, to Death.
When he wins me, filthy card,
he will scratch his gray scabs with me
and toss me away in the dung.

Also noch einen Augenblick.
Daß sie mir immer wieder den Strick
zerschneiden.
Neulich war ich so gut bereit
und es war schon ein wenig Ewigkeit
in meinen Eingeweiden.

Halten sie mir den Löffel her,
diesen Löffel Leben.
Nein ich will und ich will nicht mehr,
laßt mich mich übergeben.

Ich weiß das Leben ist gar und gut
und die Welt ist ein voller Topf,
aber mir geht es nicht ins Blut,
mir steigt es nur zu Kopf.

Andere nährt es, mich macht es krank;
begreift, daß man's verschmäht.
Mindestens ein Jahrtausend lang
brauch ich jetzt Diät.

All right now: just one last second more . . .
Thus ever again they cut
my rope.
Recently I was so prepared,
and there were even bits of eternity
in my intestines.

They hold out the spoon to me,
this spoon of life.
No, I *will* and I *will* no longer,
let me vomit up myself.

I know that life is fine and good
and the world is a full pot,
but it doesn't flow into my blood,
it only rises to my head.

Others it feeds, me it sickens;
try to understand: one *can* despise it.
For at least a thousand years now
I'll require a diet.

DAS LIED DER WITWE

Am Anfang war mir das Leben gut.
Es hielt mich warm, es machte mir Mut.
Daß es das allen Jungen tut,
wie konnt ich das damals wissen.
Ich wußte nicht, was das Leben war —,
auf einmal war es nur Jahr und Jahr,
nicht mehr gut, nicht mehr neu, nicht mehr wunderbar,
wie mitten entzwei gerissen.

Das war nicht Seine, nicht meine Schuld;
wir hatten beide nichts als Geduld,
aber der Tod hat keine.
Ich sah ihn kommen (wie schlecht er kam),
und ich schaute ihm zu wie er nahm und nahm:
es war ja gar nicht das Meine.

Was war denn das Meine; Meines, Mein?
War mir nicht selbst mein Elendsein
nur vom Schicksal geliehn?
Das Schicksal will nicht nur das Glück,
es will die Pein und das Schrein zurück
und es kauft für alt den Ruin.

Das Schicksal war da und erwarb für ein Nichts
jeden Ausdruck meines Gesichts
bis auf die Art zu gehn.
Das war ein täglicher Ausverkauf
und als ich leer war, gab es mich auf
und ließ mich offen stehn.

THE SONG OF THE WIDOW

In the beginning life was good to me.
It held me warmly, it gave me heart.
Of course it does that to all the young,
but back then how could I know?
I didn't know what living was—,
suddenly it was only year and year,
no longer bright, no longer fine, no longer magical,
as if ripped right in two.

It wasn't his, it wasn't my fault,
we both had nothing except patience,
but Death has none.
I saw him come (how meanly!)
and I watched him as he took and took:
none of it I could claim as mine.

What, then, *was* mine: mine, my own?
Was even my core of wretchedness
only lent to me by fate?
Fate wants not only the happiness,
it wants the pain and the screaming back,
and it buys the ruin second-hand.

Fate was there and obtained for a pittance
every expression of my face,
even the way I walk.
That was a daily close-out sale,
and when I was empty, it gave me up
and left me standing open.

Sie hindern mich nicht. Sie lassen mich gehn.
Sie sagen es könne nichts geschehn.
Wie gut.
Es kann nichts geschehn. Alles kommt und kreist
immerfort um den heiligen Geist,
um den gewissen Geist (du weißt) —,
wie gut.

Nein man muß wirklich nicht meinen es sei
irgend eine Gefahr dabei.
Da ist freilich das Blut.
Das Blut ist das Schwerste. Das Blut ist schwer.
Manchmal glaub ich, ich kann nicht mehr —.
(Wie gut.)

Ah was ist das für ein schöner Ball;
rot und rund wie ein Überall.
Gut, daß ihr ihn erschuft.
Ob der wohl kommt wenn man ruft?

Wie sich das alles seltsam benimmt,
ineinandertreibt, auseinanderschwimmt:
freundlich, ein wenig unbestimmt.
Wie gut.

They don't stop me. They let me go.
They say, "Nothing can happen."
How nice.
Nothing can happen. Everything comes and circles
endlessly round the Holy Ghost,
round that certain Ghost (you know)—,
how nice.

No, one really mustn't think there might be
any danger in it all.
There is of course the blood.
Blood's the hardest. Blood's like stone.
Sometimes I think I can't go on—.
(How nice.)

Ah what a lovely ball that is;
red and round like an Everywhere.
Nice that you created it.
Wonder if it comes when called?

How strangely everything behaves,
drifting together, swimming apart,
friendly, a little vague.
How nice.

Ich bin Niemand und werde auch Niemand sein.
Jetzt bin ich ja zum Sein noch zu klein;
aber auch später.

Mütter und Väter,
erbarmt euch mein.

Zwar es lohnt nicht des Pflegens Müh:
ich werde doch gemäht.
Mich kann keiner brauchen: jetzt ist es zu früh
und morgen ist es zu spät.

Ich habe nur dieses eine Kleid,
es wird dünn und es verbleicht,
aber es hält eine Ewigkeit
auch noch vor Gott vielleicht.

Ich habe nur dieses bißchen Haar
(immer dasselbe blieb),
das einmal Eines Liebstes war.

Nun hat er nichts mehr lieb.

I am Nobody and shall also be Nobody.
Now, I know, I'm still too small for being;
but later too.

Mothers and Fathers,
take pity on me.

Not that it's worth the rearing's effort:
I'll be reaped anyway.
No one can use me: today it's too early
and tomorrow too late.

I have only this one dress,
it grows thin and it turns pale,
but it will keep an eternity
even before God perhaps.

I have only this hair on my head
(always the same hair),
that was once someone's dearest love.

Now he loves nothing anymore.

Meine Seele ist vielleicht grad und gut;
aber mein Herz, mein verbogenes Blut,
alles das, was mir wehe tut,
kann sie nicht aufrecht tragen.
Sie hat keinen Garten, sie hat kein Bett,
sie hängt an meinem scharfen Skelett
mit entsetzem Flügelschlagen.

Aus meinen Händen wird auch nichts mehr.
Wie verkümmert sie sind: sieh her:
zähe hüpfen sie, feucht und schwer,
wie kleine Kröten nach Regen.
Und das Andre an mir ist
abgetragen und alt und trist;
warum zögert Gott, auf den Mist
alles das hinzulegen.

Ob er mir zürnt für mein Gesicht
mit dem mürrischen Munde?
Es war ja so oft bereit, ganz licht
und klar zu werden im Grunde;
aber nichts kam ihm je so dicht
wie die großen Hunde.
Und die Hunde haben das nicht.

My soul may be straight and good;
but my heart, my bent blood,
all that hurts me inside,
it can't hold upright.
It has no garden, it has no bed,
it clings to my sharp skeleton
with horrified beating of wings.

Nor will anything ever come of my hands.
Look at how stunted they are:
sluggishly they hop, damp and heavy,
like little toads after rain.
And the rest of me is
worn out and old and dreary;
why does God hesitate to throw
all this on the heap.

Could it be that he hates me for my face
with its grumpy jowls?
So often it was ready with all its heart
to be friendly and appealing;
but nothing ever came up close
the way the big dogs do.
And the dogs couldn't care less.

DAS LIED DES AUSSÄTZIGEN

Sieh ich bin einer, den alles verlassen hat.
Keiner weiß in der Stadt von mir,
Aussatz hat mich befallen.
Und ich schlage mein Klapperwerk,
klopfe mein trauriges Augenmerk
in die Ohren allen
die nahe vorübergehn.
Und die es hölzern hören, sehn
erst gar nicht her, und was hier geschehn
wollen sie nicht erfahren.

Soweit der Klang meiner Klapper reicht
bin ich zuhause; aber vielleicht
machst Du meine Klapper so laut,
daß sich keiner in meine Ferne traut
der mir jetzt aus der Nähe weicht.
So daß ich sehr lange gehen kann
ohne Mädchen, Frau oder Mann
oder Kind zu entdecken.

Tiere will ich nicht schrecken.

Ende des Gedicht-Kreises ›Die Stimmen‹

Look, I am one whom all have abandoned.
No one in the city knows of me,
leprosy's my lot.
And I bang my clapper
and knock the sad sight of me
into the ears of all
who come close as they pass.
And those who hear it woodenly look
this way not at all, and what happens here
they do their best not to learn.

As far as the sound of my clapper reaches
I am at home; but perhaps
You'll make my clapper so loud
that no one will dare enter my distance
who now shrinks from my nearness.
So I can go a very long way
without detecting girl, woman or man,
or even a child.

Animals I'll try not to frighten.

End of the poem cycle "The Voices"

VON DEN FONTÄNEN

Auf einmal weiß ich viel von den Fontänen,
den unbegreiflichen Bäumen aus Glas.
Ich könnte reden wie von eignen Tränen,
die ich, ergriffen von sehr großen Träumen,
einmal vergeudete und dann vergaß.

Vergaß ich denn, daß Himmel Hände reichen
zu vielen Dingen und in das Gedränge?
Sah ich nicht immer Großheit ohnegleichen
im Aufstieg alter Parke, vor den weichen
erwartungsvollen Abenden, — in bleichen
aus fremden Mädchen steigenden Gesängen,
die überfließen aus der Melodie
und wirklich werden und als müßten sie
sich spiegeln in den aufgetanen Teichen?

Ich muß mich nur erinnern an das Alles,
was an Fontänen und an mir geschah, —
dann fühl ich auch die Last des Niederfalles,
in welcher ich die Wasser wiedersah:
Und weiß von Zweigen, die sich abwärts wandten,
von Stimmen, die mit kleiner Flamme brannten,
von Teichen, welche nur die Uferkanten
schwachsinnig und verschoben wiederholten,
von Abendhimmeln, welche von verkohlten
westlichen Wäldern ganz entfremdet traten,
sich anders wölbten, dunkelten und taten
als wär das nicht die Welt, die sie gemeint . . .

Vergaß ich denn, daß Stern bei Stern versteint
und sich verschließt gegen die Nachbargloben?
Daß sich die Welten nur noch wie verweint
im Raum erkennen? — Vielleicht sind wir *oben*,

ABOUT FOUNTAINS

Suddenly I know a lot about fountains,
those incomprehensible trees of glass.
I could talk now as of my own tears,
which I, gripped by such fantastic dreaming,
spilled once and then somehow forgot.

Could I forget that the heavens reach hands
toward many things and into this commotion?
Did I not always see unrivaled greatness
in the ascent of old parks before the soft
expectant evenings—in pale chants
arising out of unknown girls
and overflowing out of the melody
and becoming real, and as if they must be
mirrored in the opened ponds?

I must only remind myself of all
that happened both with fountains and with me,—
then I feel also the weight of the descent,
in which I saw again the waters:
and know of branches that bent downwards,
of voices that burned with small flames,
of ponds that, feeble-minded and shunted off,
repeated endlessly their sharp-edged banks;
of evening skies, which from charred western forests
stepped back totally bewildered,
arched differently, darkened, and acted
as though this were not the world they had envisioned . . .

Could I forget that star flanking star grows hard
and shuts itself against its neighbor globe?
That the worlds in space only recognize each other
as if through tears?—Perhaps we are *above*,

in Himmel andrer Wesen eingewoben,
die zu uns aufschaun abends. Vielleicht loben
uns ihre Dichter. Vielleicht beten viele
zu uns empor. Vielleicht sind wir die Ziele
von fremden Flüchen, die uns nie erreichen,
Nachbaren eines Gottes, den sie meinen
in unsrer Höhe, wenn sie einsam weinen,
an den sie glauben und den sie verlieren,
und dessen Bildnis, wie ein Schein aus ihren
suchenden Lampen, flüchtig und verweht,
über unsere zerstreuten Gesichter geht . . .

woven into the skies of other beings
who gaze toward us at evening. Perhaps their
poets praise us. Perhaps some of them
pray up toward us. Perhaps we are the aim
of strange curses that never reach us,
neighbors of a god whom they envision
in our heights when they weep alone,
whom they believe in and whom they lose,
and whose image, like a gleam from their
seeking lamps, fleeting and then gone,
passes over our scattered faces . . .

DER LESENDE

Ich las schon lang. Seit dieser Nachmittag,
mit Regen rauschend, an den Fenstern lag.
Vom Winde draußen hörte ich nichts mehr:
mein Buch war schwer.
Ich sah ihm in die Blätter wie in Mienen,
die dunkel werden von Nachdenklichkeit,
und um mein Lesen staute sich die Zeit. —
Auf einmal sind die Seiten überschienen,
und statt der bangen Wortverworrenheit
steht: Abend, Abend . . . überall auf ihnen.
Ich schau noch nicht hinaus, und doch zerreißen
die langen Zeilen, und die Worte rollen
von ihren Fäden fort, wohin sie wollen . . .
Da weiß ich es: über den übervollen
glänzenden Gärten sind die Himmel weit;
die Sonne hat noch einmal kommen sollen. —
Und jetzt wird Sommernacht, soweit man sieht:
zu wenig Gruppen stellt sich das Verstreute,
dunkel, auf langen Wegen, gehn die Leute,
und seltsam weit, als ob es mehr bedeute,
hört man das Wenige, das noch geschieht.

Und wenn ich jetzt vom Buch die Augen hebe,
wird nichts befremdlich sein und alles groß.
Dort draußen ist, was ich hier drinnen lebe,
und hier und dort ist alles grenzenlos;
nur daß ich mich noch mehr damit verwebe,
wenn meine Blicke an die Dinge passen
und an die ernste Einfachheit der Massen, —
da wächst die Erde über sich hinaus.
Den ganzen Himmel scheint sie zu umfassen:
der erste Stern ist wie das letzte Haus.

THE MAN READING

I've read long now. Since this afternoon,
with its rain rushing, lay against the windows.
I'd become oblivious to the wind outside:
my book was hard.
I gazed into its lines as into faces
whose looks grow dark from deep reflection,
and around my reading the hours built up.—
Suddenly now brightness spills upon the pages,
and instead of the fearful word-confusion
stands: evening, evening . . . everywhere upon them.
I keep my eyes fixed, and yet the long lines
tear apart, and the words roll away
from their threads, to wherever they will . . .
Then I know: over the overfull
glittering gardens the skies are vast;
the sun was to have broken through once more.—
And now summer night sets in, as far as one can see:
what's dispersed collects into a few groups,
darkly, on long paths, people wander,
and strangely far-off, as if it meant more,
one hears the little that still transpires.

And when now I lift my eyes from the book,
nothing will seem alien, everything great.
There outside *exists*, what here inside I *live*,
and here and there the whole of things is boundless;
save that I weave myself still more with it
when my gaze shapes itself to objects
and to the grave simplicity of masses,—
then the earth grows out beyond itself.
It seems to encompass the entire night sky:
the first star is like the last house.

DER SCHAUENDE

Ich sehe den Bäumen die Stürme an,
die aus laugewordenen Tagen
an meine ängstlichen Fenster schlagen,
und höre die Fernen Dinge sagen,
die ich nicht ohne Freund ertragen,
nicht ohne Schwester lieben kann.

Da geht der Sturm, ein Umgestalter,
geht durch den Wald und durch die Zeit,
und alles ist wie ohne Alter:
die Landschaft, wie ein Vers im Psalter,
ist Ernst und Wucht und Ewigkeit.

Wie ist das klein, womit wir ringen,
was mit uns ringt, wie ist das groß;
ließen wir, änlicher den Dingen,
uns *so* vom großen Sturm bezwingen, —
wir würden weit und namenlos.

Was wir besiegen, ist das Kleine,
und der Erfolg selbst macht uns klein.
Das Ewige und Ungemeine
will nicht von uns gebogen sein.
Das ist der Engel, der den Ringern
des Alten Testaments erschien:
wenn seiner Widersacher Sehnen
im Kampfe sich metallen dehnen,
fühlt er sie unter seinen Fingern
wie Saiten tiefer Melodien.

Wen dieser Engel überwand,
welcher so oft auf Kampf verzichtet,
der geht gerecht und aufgerichtet

THE MAN WATCHING

I can see that the storms are coming
by the trees, which out of stale lukewarm days
beat against my anxious windows,
and I can hear the distances say things
one can't bear without a friend,
can't love without a sister.

Then the storm swirls, a rearranger,
swirls through the woods and through time,
and everything is as if without age:
the landscape, like verses in the psalter,
is weight and ardor and eternity.

How small that is, with which we wrestle,
what wrestles with us, how immense;
were we to let ourselves, the way things do,
be conquered *thus* by the great storm,—
we would become far-reaching and nameless.

What we triumph over is the Small,
and the success itself makes us petty.
The Eternal and Unexampled
will not be bent by us.
This is the Angel, who appeared
to the wrestlers of the Old Testament:
when his opponent's sinews
in that contest stretch like metal,
he feels them under his fingers
like strings making deep melodies.

Whomever this Angel overcame
(who so often declined the fight),
he walks erect and justified

und groß aus jener harten Hand,
die sich, wie formend, an ihn schmiegte.
Die Siege laden ihn nicht ein.
Sein Wachstum ist: der Tiefbesiegte
von immer Größerem zu sein.

and great out of that hard hand
which, as if sculpting, nestled round him.
Winning does not tempt him.
His growth is: to be the deeply defeated
by ever greater things.

AUS EINER STURMNACHT
Acht Blätter mit einem Titelblatt

TITELBLATT

Die Nacht, von wachsenden Sturme bewegt,
wie wird sie auf einmal weit —,
als bliebe sie sonst zusammengelegt
in die kleinlichen Falten der Zeit.
Wo die Sterne ihr wehren, dort endet sie nicht
und beginnt nicht mitten im Wald
und nicht an meinem Angesicht
und nicht mit deiner Gestalt.
Die Lampen stammeln und wissen nicht:
lügen wir Licht?
Ist die Nacht die einzige Wirklichkeit
seit Jahrtausenden . . .

FROM A STORMY NIGHT

Eight Leaves with a Title Leaf

TITLE LEAF

The night, stirred by burgeoning storms,
how it grew suddenly vast—,
as if it remains otherwise folded up
in the tiniest faults of time.
Where the stars try to stop it, it doesn't end there
and doesn't begin in the forest's depths
and not at my countenance
and not with your form.
The lamps stammer and can't be sure:
are we *lying* light?
Has night been the one reality
for thousands of years . . .

In solchen Nächten kannst du in den Gassen
Zukünftigen begegnen, schmalen blassen
Gesichtern, die dich nicht erkennen
und dich schweigend vorüberlassen.
Aber wenn sie zu reden begännen,
wärst du ein Langevergangener
wie du da stehst,
langeverwest.
Doch sie bleiben im Schweigen wie Tote,
obwohl sie die Kommenden sind.
Zukunft beginnt noch nicht.
Sie halten nur ihr Gesicht in die Zeit
und können, wie unter Wasser, nicht schauen;
und ertragen sie's doch eine Weile,
sehn sie wie unter den Wellen: die Eile
von Fischen und das Tauchen von Tauen.

Nights like these, you can meet in the streets
future people, thin pale
visages which don't recognize you
and silently let you pass.
Yet if they were to start talking,
you would be one of the long-forgotten ones,
as you stand there limply,
long-decomposed.
But they remain in the silence like the dead,
although they are the ones coming.
Future doesn't begin yet.
They hold only their faces into time
and can, as under water, not really gaze;
and if they manage to bear it a while,
they see as if under the waves: the hurry
of fishes and the diving of hawsers.

2

In solchen Nächten gehn die Gefängnisse auf.
Und durch die bösen Träume der Wächter
gehn mit leisem Gelächter
die Verächter ihrer Gewalt.
Wald! Sie kommen zu dir, um in dir zu schlafen,
mit ihren langen Strafen behangen.
    Wald!

2

Nights like these, the prison doors swing open.
And through the bad dreams of the turnkeys
file with softest laughter
the scorners of their force.
Woods! They come to you, to sleep in you,
hung with their long punishments.
   Woods!

3

In solchen Nächten ist auf einmal Feuer
in einer Oper. Wie ein Ungeheuer
beginnt der Riesenraum mit seinen Rängen
Tausende, die sich in ihm drängen,
zu kauen.
Männer und Frauen
staun sich in den Gängen,
und wie sich alle aneinander hängen,
bricht das Gemäuer, und es reißt sie mit.
Und niemand weiß mehr *wer* ganz unten litt;
während ihm einer schon das Herz zertritt,
sind seine Ohren noch ganz voll von Klängen,
die dazu hingehn . . .

3

Nights like these, there is suddenly
fire in an opera house. Like some huge monster
the cavernous space with its circles of
thousands, who crowd inside it,
starts to chew.
Women and men
jam the passageways,
and as they all cling together,
the masonry bursts, and takes them with it.
And the one farthest down hasn't a chance:
while someone's already stamped out his heart,
his ears are still full of music,
which plays as he fades . . .

4

In solchen Nächten, wie vor vielen Tagen,
fangen die *Herzen* in den Sarkophagen
vergangner Fürsten wieder an zu gehn;
und so gewaltig drängt ihr Wiederschlagen
gegen die Kapseln, welche widerstehn,
daß sie die goldnen Schalen weitertragen
durch Dunkel und Damaste, die zerfallen.
Schwarz schwankt der Dom mit allen seinen Hallen.
Die Glocken, die sich in die Türme krallen,
hängen wie Vögel, bebend stehn die Türen,
und an den Trägern zittert jedes Glied:
als trügen seinen gründenden Granit
blinde Schildkröten, die sich rühren.

4

Nights like these, as in days long past,
the *hearts* in the sarcophagi of
departed princes again start to work;
and their beating pounds with such force
against the husks, which won't open,
that they carry the golden dishes onward
through darkness and damask, which turn to dust.
The cathedral sways blackly with all its vaults.
The bells, which claw themselves into the towers,
hang like birds, the doors stand trembling,
and each strut of the buttresses shakes:
as if its great slabs of granite were borne
by blind tortoises, which begin to stir.

In solchen Nächten wissen die Unheilbaren:
wir waren . . .
Und sie denken unter den Kranken
einen einfachen guten Gedanken
weiter, dort, wo er abbrach.
Doch von den Söhnen, die sie gelassen,
geht der Jüngste vielleicht in den einsamsten Gassen;
denn gerade *diese* Nächte
sind ihm als ob er zum ersten Mal dächte:
lange lag es über ihm bleiern,
aber jetzt wird sich alles entschleiern —,
und: daß er das feiern wird,
    fühlt er . . .

5

Nights like these, the unhealable know:
we were . . .
And among the ailing they take up
some simple good thought
again, there, where it broke off.
Yet of the sons, whom they have left,
perhaps the youngest walks down the loneliest streets;
for such nights are to him
as if for the first time he had thought:
it has long covered him leadenly,
but now everything will be unveiled—,
and: so he will celebrate that,
     he feels . . .

6

In solchen Nächten sind alle die Städte gleich,
alle beflaggt.
Und an den Fahnen vom Sturm gepackt
und wie an Haaren hinausgerissen
in irgend ein Land mit ungewissen
Umrissen und Flüssen.
In allen Gärten ist dann ein Teich,
an jedem Teiche dasselbe Haus,
in jedem Hause dasselbe Licht;
und alle Menschen sehn ähnlich aus
und halten die Hände vorm Gesicht.

6

Nights like these, all the cities are the same,
all decked with flags.
And by the flags seized by the storm
and as if by hair torn away
into some country with uncertain
contours and rivers.
In all gardens then there's a pond,
by every pond the same house,
inside every house the same light;
and all the people look alike
and hold their hands in front of their faces.

7

In solchen Nächten werden die Sterbenden klar,
greifen sich leise ins wachsende Haar,
dessen Halme aus ihres Schädels Schwäche
in diesen langen Tagen *treiben*,
als wollten sie über der Oberfläche
des Todes bleiben.
Ihre Gebärde geht durch das Haus
als wenn überall Spiegel hingen;
und sie geben — mit diesem Graben
in ihren Haaren — Kräfte aus,
die sie in Jahren gesammelt haben,
    welche *vergingen*.

7

Nights like these, the dying see clearly,
reach down lightly into the growing hair
whose stalks out of their skulls' weakness
in those long hopeless days *sprout*,
as if they wanted to remain
above death's surface.
Their gesture goes through the house
as if mirrors hung everywhere;
and they give off—with this digging
into their hair—powers,
which they have gathered throughout years
     that are *gone*.

8

In solchen Nächten wächst mein Schwesterlein,
das vor mir war und vor mir starb, ganz klein.
Viel solche Nächte waren schon seither:
Sie muß schon schön sein. Bald wird irgendwer
    sie frein.

8

Nights like these, my little sister grows,
who was here and died before me, so small.
Many such nights have passed since then.
She must be beautiful by now. Soon someone
    will wed her.

DIE BLINDE

DER FREMDE:

Du bist nicht bang, davon zu sprechen?

DIE BLINDE:

Nein.

Es ist so ferne. Das war ein andre.

Die damals sah, die laut und schauend lebte,

die starb.

DER FREMDE:

Und hatte einen schweren Tod?

DIE BLINDE:

Sterben ist Grausamkeit an Ahnungslosen.

Stark muß man sein, sogar wenn Fremdes stirbt.

DER FREMDE:

Sie war dir fremd?

DIE BLINDE:

— Oder: sie ists geworden.

Der Tod entfremdet selbst dem Kind die Mutter. —

Doch es war schrecklich in den ersten Tagen.

Am ganzen Leibe war ich wund. Die Welt,

die in den Dingen blüht und reift,

war mit den Wurzeln aus mir ausgerissen,

mit meinem Herzen (schien mir), und ich lag

wie aufgewühlte Erde offen da und trank

den kalten Regen meiner Tränen,

der aus den toten Augen unaufhörlich

und leise strömte, wie aus leeren Himmeln,

wenn Gott gestorben ist, die Wolken fallen.

Und mein Gehör war groß und allem offen.

Ich hörte Dinge, die nicht hörbar sind:

die Zeit, die über meine Haare floß,

die Stille, die in zarten Gläsern klang, —

und fühlte: nah bei meinen Händen ging

der Atem einer großen weißen Rose.

THE BLIND WOMAN

THE STRANGER:
   You aren't afraid to speak of it?
THE BLIND WOMAN:
   No.
   It's so far away. That was someone else.
   Who saw back then, who lived aloud and looking,
   who died.
THE STRANGER:
   And died a hard death?
THE BLIND WOMAN:
   Dying's cruel to the unsuspecting.
   One must be strong even when strangers die.
THE STRANGER:
   She was a stranger to you?
THE BLIND WOMAN:
   —Or: she has become so.
   Death estranges even the child from the mother.
   But it was terrible in those first days.
   My entire body was a wound. The world
   that blooms and ripens in things
   had been torn out of me with its roots,
   with my heart (it seemed), and I lay
   like churned-up earth and drank
   the cold raining of my tears,
   which out of dead eyes ceaselessly
   and softly streamed, the way from empty heavens,
   when God has died, the clouds fall.
   And my hearing was open to everything.
   I heard things that are not audible:
   time, which flowed over my hair,
   stillness, which rang in thinnest crystal,—
   and felt: close to my hand the breath
   of a great white rose went past.

Und immer wieder dacht ich: Nacht und: Nacht
und glaubte einen hellen Streif zu sehn,
der wachsen würde wie ein Tag;
und glaubte auf den Morgen zuzugehn,
der längst in meinen Händen lag.
Die Mutter weckt ich, wenn der Schlaf mir schwer
hinunterfiel vom dunklen Gesicht,
der Mutter rief ich: »Du, komm her!
Mach Licht!«
Und horchte. Lange, lange blieb es still,
und meine Kissen fühlte ich versteinen, —
dann wars, als säh ich etwas scheinen:
das war der Mutter wehes Weinen,
an das ich nicht mehr denken will.
Mach Licht! Mach Licht! Ich schrie es oft im Traum:
Der Raum ist eingefallen. Nimm den Raum
mir vom Gesicht und von der Brust.
Du mußt ihn heben, hochheben,
mußt ihn wieder den Sternen geben;
ich kann nicht leben so, mit dem Himmel auf mir.
Aber sprech ich zu dir, Mutter?
Oder zu wem denn? Wer ist denn dahinter?
Wer ist denn hinter dem Vorhang? — Winter?
Mutter: Sturm? Mutter: Nacht? Sag!
Oder: Tag? . . . Tag!
Ohne micht! Wie kann es denn ohne mich Tag sein?
Fehl ich denn nirgends?
Fragt denn niemand nach mir?
Sind wir denn ganz vergessen?
Wir? . . . Aber du bist ja dort;
du hast ja noch alles, nicht?
Um dein Gesicht sind noch alle Dinge bemüht,
ihm wohlzutun.
Wenn deine Augen ruhn
und wenn sie noch so müd waren,
sie können wieder steigen.

And over and over I thought: *night* and: *night*
and believed I saw a bright strip
that would fan out like a day;
and believed I neared the morning
that had long rested in my hands.
I woke my mother when sleep slowly
fell down off my dark face,
I called to her: "Mother, come quickly!
Bring light!"
And listened. Long, long, it was silent,
and I felt my pillows turn to stone,—
then it was as if I saw something shine:
it was my mother's grief-filled weeping,
about which I no longer wish to think.
Bring light! Bring light! I screamed it in dreams:
Space has caved in. Take the space
off my face and off my breast.
You must lift it, lift it up high,
must give it back to the stars;
I can't live like this, with the sky upon me.
But do I speak to you, Mother?
Or to whom? Who is over there?
Who stands behind the curtain? —Winter?
Mother: Storm? Mother: Night? Say something!
Or else: Day? . . . Day!
Without me! How can it be day without me?
Am I missed nowhere?
Does no one ask about me?
Are we entirely forgotten?
We? . . . But you're there;
you still have everything, no?
All things still busily attend your sight,
caring for its needs.
When your eyes rest,
and no matter how tired they were,
they can still rise again.

235

... Meine schweigen.

Meine Blumen werden die Farbe verlieren.

Meine Spiegel werden zufrieren.

In meinen Büchern werden die Zeilen verwachsen.

Meine Vögel werden in den Gassen

herumflattern und sich an fremden Fenstern verwunden.

Nichts ist mehr mit mir verbunden.

Ich bin von allem verlassen. —

Ich bin eine Insel.

DER FREMDE:

Und ich bin über das Meer gekommen.

DIE BLINDE:

Wie? Auf die Insel? ... Hergekommen?

DER FREMDE:

Ich bin noch im Kahne.

Ich habe ihn leise angelegt —

an dich. Er ist bewegt:

seine Fahne weht landein.

DIE BLINDE:

Ich bin eine Insel und allein.

Ich bin reich. —

Zuerst, als die alten Wege noch waren

in meinen Nerven, ausgefahren

von vielem Gebrauch:

da litt ich auch.

Alles ging mir aus dem Herzen fort,

ich wußte erst nicht wohin;

aber dann fand ich sie alle dort,

alle Gefühle, das, was ich bin,

stand versammelt und drängte und schrie

an den vermauerten Augen, die sich nicht rührten.

Alle meine verführten Gefühle ...

Ich weiß nicht, ob sie Jahre so standen,

aber ich weiß von den Wochen,

da sie alle zurückkamen gebrochen

und niemanden erkannten.

. . . Mine are silent.
My flowers will lose their colors.
My mirrors will freeze over.
In my books the lines will run together.
My birds will flutter in the narrow streets
and hurt themselves at unknown windows.
Nothing is joined with me anymore.
All have abandoned me.
I am an island.

THE STRANGER:

And I have come across the sea.

THE BLIND WOMAN:

What? To the island? . . . Journeyed here?

THE STRANGER:

I am still in the skiff.
I have lightly berthed it—
next to you. It rocks gently:
its flag blows landward.

THE BLIND WOMAN:

I am an island and alone.
I am rich.—
At first, when the old paths were still
in my nerves, well-marked
from so much use:
then I suffered too.
Everything in my heart went away,
I didn't know at first where to search;
but then I found them all there,
all my feelings, all that I am,
stood together and thronged and screamed
at the walled-up eyes, which refused to move.
All my led-astray feelings . . .
I don't know if they'd stood like that for years,
but I remember the weeks
when they all came back broken
and recognized no one.

Dann wuchs der Weg zu den Augen zu.
Ich weiß ihn nicht mehr.
Jetzt geht alles in mir umher,
sicher und sorglos; wie Genesende
gehn die Gefühle, genießend das Gehn,
durch meines Leibes dunkles Haus.
Einige sind Lesende
über Erinnerungen;
aber die jungen
sehn alle hinaus.
Denn wo sie hintreten an meinen Rand,
ist mein Gewand von Glas.
Meine Stirne sieht, meine Hand las
Gedichte in anderen Händen.
Mein Fuß spricht mit den Steinen, die er betritt,
meine Stimme nimmt jeder Vogel mit
aus den täglichen Wänden.
Ich muß nichts mehr entbehren jetzt,
alle Farben sind übersetzt
in Geräusch und Geruch.
Und sie klingen unendlich schön
als Töne.
Was soll mir ein Buch?
In den Bäumen blättert der Wind;
und ich weiß, was dorten für Worte sind,
und wiederhole sie manchmal leis.
Und der Tod, der Augen wie Blumen bricht,
findet meine Augen nicht . . .

DER FREMDE *leise*:
   Ich weiß.

Then the path to my eyes grew over.
I no longer know where it is.
Now everything moves about in me
confident and carefree; like convalescents
my feelings move, enjoying the walk
through my body's dark house.
A few like to read
about memories;
but the young ones
all look out.
And wherever they step toward my edge,
my garment is of glass.
My brow sees, my hand reads
poems in other hands.
My foot talks with the stones it treads,
my voice flies out with every bird
beyond the daily walls.
I no longer have to do without now,
all colors are translated
into sounds and smells.
And they ring infinitely sweet
like tones.
Why should I need a book?
The wind leafs through the trees;
and I know what passes there for words,
and sometimes repeat them softly.
And Death, who plucks eyes like flowers,
doesn't find my eyes . . .

THE STRANGER *softly*:
    I know.

REQUIEM
Clara Westhoff gewidmet

Seit einer Stunde ist um ein Ding mehr
auf Erden. Mehr um einen Kranz.
Vor einer Weile war das leichtes Laub . . . Ich wands:
Und jetzt ist dieser Efeu seltsam schwer
und so von Dunkel voll, als tränke er
aus meinen Dingen zukünftige Nächte.
Jetzt graut mir fast vor dieser nächsten Nacht,
allein mit diesem Kranz, den ich gemacht,
nicht ahnend, daß da etwas wird,
wenn sich die Ranken ründen um den Reifen;
ganz nur bedürftig, dieses zu begreifen:
daß etwas nichtmehr sein kann. Wie verirrt
in nie betretene Gedanken, darinnen wunderliche Dinge stehn,
die ich schon einmal gesehen haben muß . . .

. . . Flußabwärts treiben die Blumen, welche die Kinder gerissen
haben im Spiel; aus den offenen Fingern fiel eine und eine, bis daß der
Strauß nicht mehr zu erkennen war. Bis der Rest, den sie nachhaus
gebracht, gegrade gut zum verbrennen war. Dann konnte man ja die
ganze Nacht, wenn einen alle schlafen meinen, um die gebrochenen
Blumen weinen.

Gretel, von allem Anbeginn
war dir bestimmt, sehr zeitig zu sterben,
blond zu sterben.
Lange schon, eh dir zu leben bestimmt war.
Darum stellte der Herr eine Schwester vor dich
und dann einen Bruder,
damit vor dir wären zwei Nahe, zwei Reine,
welche das Sterben dir zeigten,
das deine:
dein Sterben.

REQUIEM
Dedicated to Clara Westhoff

An hour since, now, there is more on earth
by one thing. More by a wreath.
Earlier it was light leaves . . . I turned it:
and now this ivy is oddly heavy
and so full of darkness, as if it drank
future nights out of my things.
Now I almost dread the next night
alone with this wreath that I fashioned,
not suspecting that something enters existence
when the tendrils coil around the hoop;
wholly needing to grasp just this:
that something can be no more. As if astray
in never entered thoughts, where marvelous things stand,
which somehow I must have seen before . . .

. . . Downstream drift flowers that children tore off in play; out of
their open fingers fell one, then another, until the bouquet had lost all
shape. Until the remnant they brought home was only fit to burn.
Then of course the whole night, when they all think one asleep, one
could weep for the broken flowers.

Gretel, from earliest beginning
it was doomed that you should die so early,
die fair.
Long before you were doomed to live.
For that the Lord placed a sister ahead of you
and then a brother,
so that ahead of you would be two near, two pure ones,
who would show dying to you,
show you your own:
your dying.

Deine Geschwister wurden erfunden
nur, damit du dich dran gewöhntest,
und dich an zweien Sterbestunden
mit der dritten versöhntest,
die dir seit Jahrtausenden droht.
Für deinen Tod
sind Leben erstanden;
Hände, welche Blüten banden,
Blicke, welche die Rosen rot
und die Menschen mächtig empfanden,
hat man gebildet und wieder vernichtet
und hat zweimal das Sterben *gedichtet,*
eh es, gegen dich selbst gerichtet,
aus der verloschenen Bühne trat.

. . . Nahte es dir schrecklich, geliebte Gespielin?
war es dein Feind?
Hast du dich ihm ans Herz geweint?
Hat es dich aus den heißen Kissen
in die flackernde Nacht gerissen,
in der niemand schlief im ganzen Haus . . . ?
Wie sah es aus?
Du mußt es wissen . . .
Du bist dazu in die Heimat gereist.

––––––––––––––––––––

Du weißt
wie die Mandeln blühn
und daß Seeen blau sind.
Viele Dinge, die nur im Gefühle der Frau sind
welche die erste Liebe erfuhr, —
weißt du. Dir flüsterte die Natur
in des Südens spätdämmernden Tagen
so unendliche Schönheit ein,
wie sonst nur selige Lippen sie sagen
seliger Menschen, die zu zwein

Your sister and brother were invented
only so that you might get used to it
and by means of two death-bed hours
reconcile yourself to that third
which for millenniums has threatened you.
For your death,
lives came into being;
hands, which tied blossoms,
eyes, which felt roses redly
and mankind massively,
were fashioned and again destroyed,
and twice the act of dying was *performed*,
until, aimed at you yourself,
it stepped from the extinguished stage.

. . . Was its nearing frightful, dearest playmate?
was it your foe?
Did you weep yourself to its heart?
Did it tear you out of the burning pillows
into the flickering night where
no one in the whole house slept . . . ?
How did it look?
You must know . . .
It was for that you journeyed home.

— — — — — — — — — — — — — — — — — — — —

You know
how the almond trees bloom
and that lakes are blue.
Many things that exist only in the feelings
of a woman who has known first love,—
you know. To you Nature kept whispering
in the South's late-fading days
beauty so infinite
that only the blissful lips
of blissful pairs can speak it, who, as two together,

eine Welt haben und *eine* Stimme —
leiser hast du das alles gespürt, —
(o wie hat das unendlich Grimme
deine unendliche Demut berührt).
Deine Briefe kamen von Süden,
warm noch von Sonne, aber verwaist, —
endlich bist du selbst deinen müden
bittenden Briefen nachgereist;
denn du warst nicht gerne im Glanze,
jede Farbe lag auf dir wie Schuld,
und du lebtest in Ungeduld,
denn du wußtest: das ist nicht *das Ganze*.
Leben ist nur ein Teil . . . Wovon?
Leben ist nur ein Ton . . . Worin?
Leben hat Sinn nur, verbunden mit vielen
Kreisen des weithin wachsenden Raumes, —
Leben ist so nur der Traum eines Traumes,
aber Wachsein ist anderswo.
So ließest du's los.
Groß ließest du's los.
Und wir kannten dich klein.
Dein war so wenig: ein Lächeln, ein kleines,
ein bißchen melancholisch schon immer,
sehr sanftes Haar und ein kleines Zimmer,
das dir seit dem Tode der Schwester weitwar.
Als ob alles andere nur dein Kleid war
so scheint es mir jetzt, du stilles Gespiel.
Aber *sehr viel*
warst du. Und wir wußtens manchmal,
wenn du am Abend kamst in den Saal;
wußten manchmal: jetzt müßte man beten;
eine Menge ist eingetreten,
eine Menge, welche dir nachgeht,
weil du den Weg weißt.
Und du hast ihn wissen gemußt
und hast ihn gewußt

have *one* world and *one* voice—
more subtly you've traced all that,—
(O how the infinitely grim
touched your infinite humility).
Your letters arrived from the South,
still warm from the sun, but orphaned,—
at last you yourself followed your
tired beseeching letters;
for you were not happy in all that brilliance,
every color lay on you like guilt,
and you lived in impatience,
for you knew: this is not *the whole.*
Life is only a part . . . of what?
Life is only a note . . . in what?
Life has meaning only joined with many
receding circles of increasing space,—
life is only the dream of a dream,
but waking is elsewhere.
So you let it go.
Greatly you let it go.
And we knew you as someone small.
There was so little of you: a smile, a small one,
a bit melancholy always,
the softest hair and a small room
that since your sister's death seemed huge to you.
As if all else was just your dress
it now seems to me, you silent playmate.
But how very much
you *were.* And we knew it sometimes,
when toward evening you came into the room;
knew sometimes: now one must pray;
a multitude has entered,
a multitude that follows you,
because you know the way.
And you had to have known it
and did know it

gestern . . .
jüngste der Schwestern.

Sieh her,
dieser Kranz ist so schwer.
Und sie werden ihn auf dich legen,
diesen schweren Kranz.
Kanns dein Sarg aushalten?
Wenn er bricht
unter dem schwarzen Gewicht,
kriecht in die Falten
von deinem Kleid
Efeu.
Weit rankt er hinauf,
rings rankt er dich um,
und der Saft, der sich in seinen Ranken bewegt,
regt dich auf mit seinem Geräusch;
so keusch bist du.
Aber du bist nichtmehr zu.
Langgedehnt bist du und laß.
Deines Leibes Türen sind angelehnt,
und naß
tritt der Efeu ein . . .

— — — — — — — — — — —

wie Reihn
von Nonnen,
die sich führen
an schwarzem Seil,
weil es dunkel ist in dir, du Bronnen.
In den leeren Gängen
deines Blutes drängen sie zu deinem Herzen;
wo sonst deine sanften Schmerzen
sich begegneten mit bleichen
Freuden und Erinnerungen, —
wandeln sie, wie im Gebet,

246

yesterday . . .
youngest of the sisters.

See here,
this wreath is so heavy.
And they will lay it down on you,
this heavy wreath.
Can your coffin bear it?
When it breaks
under the black weight,
into the folds of your dress
will creep
ivy.
Far up it will twine,
it will twine up all around you
and the sap that stirs in its tendrils
will arouse you with its noise;
so chaste are you.
But you are closed no longer.
You are stretched out limp and lax.
Your body's doors are left ajar,
and damply
the ivy enters . . .

— — — — — — — — —

like rows
of nuns
who guide themselves
along a black rope,
since it is dark in you, you well.
Through the empty corridors
of your blood they press on toward your heart;
where once your gentle sorrows
met with pale
joys and remembrances,—
they wander, as if in prayer,

in das Herz, das, ganz verklungen,
dunkel, allen offen steht.

Aber dieser Kranz ist schwer
nur im Licht,
nur unter Lebenden, hier bei mir;
und sein Gewicht
ist nicht mehr
wenn ich ihn, zu dir legen werde.
Die Erde ist voller Gleichgewicht,
Deine Erde.
Er ist schwer von meinen Augen, die daran hängen,
schwer von den Gängen,
die ich um ihn getan;
Ängste aller, welche ihn sahn,
haften daran.
Nimm ihn zu dir, denn er ist dein
seit er ganz fertig ist.
Nimm ihn von mir.
Laß mich allein! Er ist wie ein Gast . . .
fast schäm ich mich seiner.
Hast du auch Furcht, Gretel?

Du kannst nicht mehr gehn?
Kannst nicht mehr bei mir in der Stube stehn?
Tun dir die Füße weh?
So bleib wo jetzt alle beisammen sind,
man wird ihn dir morgen bringen, mein Kind,
durch die entlaubte Allee.
Man wird ihn dir bringen, warte getrost, —
man bringt dir morgen noch mehr.
Wenn es auch morgen tobt und tost,
das schadet den Blumen nicht sehr.
Man wird sie dir bringen. Du hast das Recht,
sie sicher zu haben, mein Kind,
und wenn sie auch morgen schwarz und schlecht

into your heart, which, completely soundless,
darkened, to all stands open.

But this wreath is heavy
only in the light,
only among the living, here with me;
and its weight
will cease
when I place it next to you.
The earth is full of balance,
Your earth.
The wreath is heavy from my eyes, which hang on it,
heavy from the walking
that I did for it;
fears of everyone who saw it
cling to it.
Take it to you, for it is yours
since it is finished now.
Take it away from me.
Let me be alone! It is like a guest . . .
I'm almost ashamed of it.
Are you afraid too, Gretel?

You can walk no longer?
No longer stand here in my room?
Do your feet hurt you?
Then stay where now all are together,
it will be brought to you tomorrow, my child,
through the leaf-stripped avenue.
It will be brought to you, wait with good cheer,—
you will be brought that and more.
Even if tomorrow it storms and rages,
that won't harm the flowers much.
They will be brought to you. It is your right
to have them as your own, my child,
and even if tomorrow they are black and ruined

und lange vergangen sind.
Sei deshalb nicht bange. Du wirst nicht mehr
unterscheiden, was steigt oder sinkt;
die Farben sind zu und die Töne sind leer,
und du wirst auch gar nicht mehr wissen, wer
dir alle die Blumen bringt.

Jetzt weißt du *das Andre*, das uns verstößt,
so oft wir's im Dunkel erfaßt;
von dem, was du *sehntest*, bist du erlöst
zu etwas, was du *hast*.
Unter uns warst du von kleiner Gestalt,
vielleicht bist du jetzt ein erwachsener Wald
mit Winden und Stimmen im Laub. —
Glaub mir, Gespiel, dir geschah nicht Gewalt:
Dein Tod war schon alt,
als dein Leben begann;
drum griff er es an,
damit es ihn nicht überlebte.
. . . .

Schwebte etwas um mich?
Trat Nachtwind herein?
Ich bebte nicht.
Ich bin stark und allein. —
Was hab ich heute geschafft?
. . . Efeulaub holt ich am Abend und wands
und bog es zusammen, bis es ganz gehorchte.
Noch glänzt es mit schwarzem Glanz.
Und meine Kraft
kreist in dem Kranz.

and have been dead a long time.
Don't let that frighten you: you won't distinguish
any longer what rises from what sets;
the colors are closed, the sounds are empty,
and you won't even know any longer
who brings you all the flowers.

Now you know *that other*, which disowns us
whenever we grasp it in the dark;
from that which you *desired*, you've been released
to something that you *have*.
Among us you were small of stature,
perhaps you are now a full-grown forest
with winds and voices in your boughs.—
Believe me, playmate, no violence was done to you:
Your death was old already
when your life began;
therefore he attacked it,
lest it outlive him.

· ·

Did something hover round me?
Did nightwind enter?
I didn't tremble.
I am steadfast and alone.—
What have I made today?
. . . I fetched ivy at evening and turned it
and twisted it together, until it utterly obeyed.
It still shines with black light.
And my strength
spirals in the wreath.

SCHLUSZSTÜCK

Der Tod ist groß.
Wir sind die Seinen
lachenden Munds.
Wenn wir uns mitten im Leben meinen,
wagt er zu weinen
mitten in uns.

CLOSING PIECE

Death is great.
We are his completely
with laughing eyes.
When we feel ourselves immersed in life,
he dares to weep
immersed in us.

NOTES

page 5, "Entrance." Untitled in the 1902 edition.

page 7, "From an April." Untitled in the 1902 edition.

page 9, "Two Poems to Hans Thomas on His Sixtieth Birthday." Hans Thomas: a painter and illustrator (1839–1924) popular in his time for his almost childlike depictions of landscapes and human figures. "Mondnacht" probably alludes to a painting by Thomas entitled *Der Mondscheingeiger*; "Ritter" perhaps to the artist's *Einsamer Ritt*.

page 15, "Girls." The two parts are separate and untitled in the 1902 edition.

page 57, "Initial." Untitled in the 1902 edition. Listed in the table of contents as "Connecting Piece" (*Zwischenstück*).

page 65, "Pont du Carrousel." Pont du Carrousel: a bridge over the Seine, to the Place du Carrousel in Paris.

page 69, "The Ashanti." Jardin d'Acclimatation: an amusement park with zoo in the Bois de Bologne, Paris. Ashanti: a region in Africa now part of the Republic of Ghana; here signifying inhabitants of or from that region.

page 73, "Apprehension." Untitled in the 1902 edition.

page 75, "Lament." Untitled in the 1902 edition.

page 95, "Storm." Mazeppa: a cossack leader ("hetman") who joined his forces with the invading Swedish army led by Charles XII in the Battle of Poltava, fought in the Ukraine in 1709 and won by the Russians under Peter the Great. Regarded by some as a political opportunist and by others as a patriot dedicated to freeing his native Ukraine, he became a charismatic figure in the European imagination. Rilke's poem shifts abruptly from the Mazeppa of history to the Mazeppa of popular legend to produce its own epiphany. According to one well-known "Byronic" anecdote, Mazeppa was caught in bed with the wife of a Polish nobleman, and as punishment was strapped naked to the back of a wild horse and sent galloping off into the steppe.

page 97, "Evening in Skåne." Skåne: southern region of Sweden, where Rilke stayed for a time as guest of Hanna Larsson and her fiancé (the artist and writer Ernst Norlind) at her country estate at Borgeby Gård.

page 107, "Initial." Untitled in the 1902 edition. Listed as "Connecting Piece" (*Zwischenstück*) in the table of contents.

page 117, "In the Certosa." Certosa: Carthusian monastery. La Stanca: It., "the tired one." Pietrabianca: It., "white stone," here used as a place name.

page 131, "Charles the Twelfth of Sweden Rides in the Ukraine." The first part ("Kings in legends . . . ") is separate and untitled in the 1902 edition. Charles the Twelfth: king of Sweden from 1682 to 1718. His defeat at the Battle of Poltava (1709) marked the turning point in the long "Northern War" between Russia and Sweden (1700–1721). *Geschlagen* in line 2 of the main section of Rilke's poem can mean "beaten," "struck" or "smitten" (in the biblical sense), or "killed." The narrative plays among these meanings.

page 137, "The Son." The second part (" . . . Thus we became . . . ") is separate and untitled in the 1902 edition.

page 143, "The Tsars: A Poem Cycle (1899 and 1906)." All these poems except the third belong to the period between Rilke's two Russian journeys (April 25–June 18, 1899, and May 7–August 24, 1900). The third (which indeed feels very different in spirit) dates from early February 1906. The second, fifth, and sixth were revised during that same period. For much of the information in the following notes I am indebted to Patricia Pollock Brodsky, *Russia in the Works of Rainer Maria Rilke* (Detroit: Wayne State University Press, 1984), 88–95.

I. "That was in days when the mountains came." The subject of this and the following poem is Ilya Muromets, a legendary figure from the Russian medieval epics, the *byliny*. Ilya of Muron, the only son of a well-to-do farmer, was crippled and somnolent from birth. One day when his parents were at work in the field, two pilgrims entered the hut where he slept and offered him a drink. Suddenly he could stand erect, and felt himself infused with superhuman strength. Following the pilgrims' orders, he went out into the field to help his parents, then bought a suit of armor and a gray stallion, and embarked on a series of adventures that led him to the court of Prince Vladimir of Kiev, the tenth-century Christianizer of Russia.

II. "Great birds still threaten on all sides." The starting-point for this poem is Ilya's battle with and capture of Solovey-Razboynik ("Nightingale-the-Robber"), who lurks in the tops of many oaks in the dark forest of Bryn, swooping down on unwary travelers (for thirty years no one has been allowed to pass). In the legends Solovey is portrayed as earthy and folksy, a semihuman trickster or peasant-robber. The power of his cry is always stressed: once it even blows the roof off

Prince Vladimir's palace. Rilke translates all this rather quaint material into an abstruse metaphysical language, which attempts to describe both the terrors of a "prehistoric" spring bursting with voice and transformation, and its downfall in confrontation with the "staying-power" of the first heroes of civilization.

III. "His servants feed with more and more." The subject of this poem is Ivan the Terrible, a paranoid psychopath who ruled as Tsar from 1547 to 1584, strengthening the empire and sowing the seeds of its decline. Rilke sketches Ivan's madness with a series of oblique details. The "murderers" who "play the monk" are the *oprichniki*, a personal guard Ivan formed in 1565 out of the most hardened criminals in Russia. For a time he moved with three hundred of these guards into a fortress outside Moscow, had them dress in monks' habits, and established a monastic rule that mixed sexual orgies and sick religiosity. "The iron on his stick" recalls the fit of rage in which Ivan struck and killed with his iron-tipped cane his best-loved son, Ivan.

IV. "It is the hour when the empire vainly." The subject of the last three poems is Feodor, the feeble-minded son of Ivan the Terrible, and the last of the Rurik line.

VI. "Still in the surrounding silver-plating." Icons in the Russian Orthodox Church were often covered over with gold or silver plating, into which holes were cut to let the face and hands of the underlying figure show through. The metal itself (in contrast to the austerity of the image) was often elaborately ornamented.

page 167, "The Singer Sings Before a Child of Princes." Paula Becker-Modersohn died on November 20, 1907. (Her death occasioned one of Rilke's greatest poems, the "Requiem for a Friend" of 1908.) The dedication first appeared in the fifth edition of *The Book of Images*, published in 1913. But a letter from Rilke to Paula of 5 November 1900 makes clear that the poem was written from the first with her in mind: "Next time I shall copy out for you the song: 'You pale child, each evening shall . . . ,' and send you this poem. It does not really exist if you do not possess it—for, after all, it so to speak began with you."

page 173, "Those of the House of Colonna." Colonna: the name of an aristocratic Italian family which between the twelfth and sixteenth centuries played a dominant role in the history and politics of Rome. This poem is contemporaneous (Rome, late 1903/early 1904) with three of the earliest of the *New Poems*: "Hetaerae-Tombs," "Orpheus. Eurydice. Hermes," and "Birth of Venus."

page 185, "The Voices." These poems, written in early June of 1906, when Rilke was in Paris working on the *New Poems* and *The Notebooks of Malte Laurids Brigge*, were the last composed for *The Book of Images*. Rilke sent them to his publisher with a note expressing hope that they would prevent the volume as a whole from being "purely aesthetic."

page 241, "Requiem." On November 20, 1900, Rilke received news from Clara Westhoff (whom he would marry in March 1901) that her friend Gretel Kottmeyer had died. (The dedication in the 1902 edition reads "For Gretel. Dedicated to Clara Westhoff.") He paraphrased her letter in his diary:

Clara W. writes today about a black ivy-wreath, and what she relates is already a poem in its own right. How she speaks of this heavy black wreath which she took unsuspectingly from the gable of her house out of the gray November air and which then became so monstrously serious in the room, a thing unto itself, a thing more suddenly, and a thing which seemed to become constantly heavier, drinking up all the sorrowing in the air of the room and the early dawn. And all this then shall lie on the thin wooden coffin of the poor girl who has died in the South. . . . The black wreath will perhaps impress itself on the coffin, and its long roots will crawl up the white shroud and grow into the folded hands and grow into the never-loved hair and grow into the heart which, full of clogged blood, has also become black and flat and in the twilight of the dead one will scarcely be distinguishable from the heartlike leaves of the ivy. . . . And through the empty corridors of the blood the ivy will go, leaf upon leaf on its long roots, like nuns who lead one another along a single rope and who pilgrimage to the deceased heart, whose doors are only slightly left ajar.

To this entry Rilke adds a postscript: "I would like to write a requiem with this image." That Rilke imagines the poem as spoken by Clara herself is made clear in a parenthetical remark in his letter to her of February 9, 1902: ". . . like the poet of the Requiem, who indeed you yourself are."